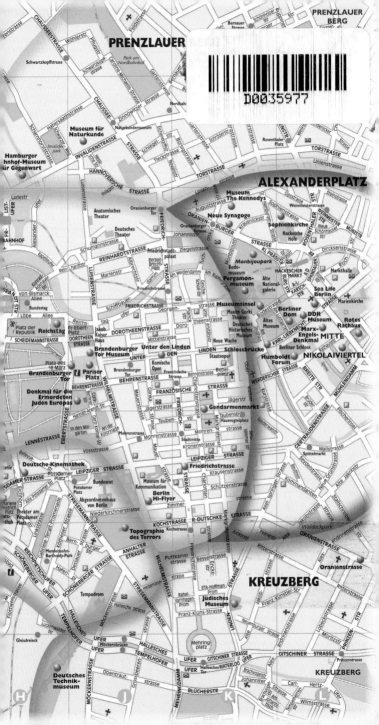

BERLIN

How to Use This Book

KEY TO SYMBOLS

➕ Map reference to the accompanying fold-out map

✉ Address

☎ Telephone number

🕔 Opening/closing times

🍴 Restaurant or café

🚆 Nearest rail station

Ⓜ Nearest subway (Metro) station

🚌 Nearest bus route

🚢 Nearest riverboat or ferry stop

♿ Facilities for visitors with disabilities

❓ Other practical information

▷ Further information

ℹ Tourist information

✋ Admission charges:
Expensive (more than €8)
Moderate (€4–€8)
Inexpensive (€4 or less)

This guide is divided into four sections

● Essential Berlin: An introduction to the city and tips on making the most of your stay.
● Berlin by Area: We've broken the city into eight areas, and recommended the best sights, shops, entertainment venues, nightlife and restaurants in each one. Suggested walks help you to explore on foot.
● Where to Stay: The best hotels, whether you're looking for luxury, budget or something in between.
● Need to Know: The info you need to make your trip run smoothly, including getting about by public transportation, weather tips, emergency phone numbers and useful websites.

Navigation In the Berlin by Area chapter, we've given each area of the city its own color, which is also used on the locator maps throughout the book and the map on the inside front cover.

Maps The fold-out map with this book is a comprehensive street plan of Berlin. The grid on this fold-out map is the same as the grid on the locator maps within the book. We've given grid references within the book for each sight and listing.

Contents

CONTENTS

Introducing Berlin

Berlin likes to think of itself as a *Weltstadt* (world city), an energetic European capital that is going places. Exciting, liberal and open, this is a city where there is always something going on—for everyone.

What is Berlin? The city is not easy to describe in words; it's the capital of a reunified federal Germany, but that reveals little. A place of baleful recollection and courageous defiance, all in living memory, but that doesn't tell you about right now. A vast studio for artists and a building site for entrepreneurs and government departments—that says more.

Berlin is a stroll through the green hectares of the Grunewald and the Tiergarten, and a sober walk around the grim obstacle course of the Holocaust Memorial. It is a café terrace on the banks of the Spree and a Turkish coffee house in Kreuzberg; a designer shopping expedition on Ku'damm and a stroll around the New Age shops in Prenzlauer Berg; a night at the Deutsche Oper and an ear-splitting rave at the repurposed brewery now dubbed the KulturBrauerei. Berlin can be both *gemütlich* (comfortable) and hard-edged, sentimental and sardonic, cultivated and raucous, multicultural and narrow-minded. In a sense this city is still divided into East and West, not by a physical wall but by a slowly fading line in its psyche.

Alternative lifestyles abound. Cabaret is going strong, and transvestite shows are legion. Visitors pour in for the Christopher Street Day gay and lesbian festival or the *Karneval der Kulturen,* as well as for business conventions. An exuberant feeling of something new abounds, an energy that needs to find an outlet, and Berlin has plenty of those.

Above all, Berlin is once again where it was destined to be: one of the great European capitals, warts and all.

FACTS AND FIGURES

- The population of Berlin is 3.7 million.
- 49 percent of the population is male; 51 percent female.
- 14 percent are foreign nationals; 12 percent belong to an ethnic minority, a third of them Turkish.
- 19 percent are Protestants, 9 percent Catholics, 8 percent Muslim and most of the rest claim no religious affiliation.

HEART TRANSPLANT

A new city heart has emerged between Potsdamer Platz and the government district along the former East–West border. Completely destroyed during World War II, this area was the biggest building site in Europe during the 1990s. Today, it is a bustling entertainment and business district, reflecting Berlin's modern architectural face.

THE CÖLLN WALL?

Medieval Cölln, on the River Spree's south bank, was founded in 1237, seven years before Berlin on the north bank. The two sister towns developed side by side until 1710, when Cölln was subsumed into Berlin. If it had gone the other way, which could so easily have happened, Germany's capital would be known today as Cölln, not to be confused with Köln (Cologne).

FRESH AIR

Nearly a third of Berlin consists of parks, meadows, woodland, lakes (Berlin is surrounded by lakes) and rivers. There are more than 16,000ha (39,500 acres) of woodland inside the city. Parks, castle grounds, zoos and botanical gardens all provide spaces for relaxation and trees to keep the city air relatively clean—although pollution is still an issue here.

A Short Stay in Berlin

DAY 1

Morning Start the day with a stroll through the **Tiergarten** (▷ 66–67). Aim to end at the **Brandenburger Tor** (▷ 60), from where you can easily reach the **Reichstag** (▷ 65), seat of the federal German parliament.

Mid-morning Go south, taking in the grim spectacle of the **Denkmal für die Ermordeten Juden Europas** (▷ 69) monument along the way, to the imposing **Potsdamer Platz** (▷ 39–48). From here it's not far along Potsdamer Strasse to the **Gemäldegalerie** (▷ 42–43) for a session of serious art appreciation.

Lunch To be kind to your feet at this point, go up onto Tiergarten Strasse and take bus 200 west to Breitscheidplatz. Then cross over to **Kurfürstendamm** (▷ 33). For a light lunch, choose either **Soupkultur** (▷ 38), or one of the great snack bars inside **KaDeWe** (▷ 36).

Afternoon Backtrack the short distance to Breitscheidplatz for a close-up look at the bomb-blasted **Kaiser-Wilhelm-Gedächtniskirche** (▷ 32), and pass a few moments in quiet contemplation in its memorial chapel.

Mid-afternoon Either walk via side streets, or take bus M45 northwest to Luisenplatz. From here you can visit ornate **Schloss Charlottenburg** (▷ 24–25). Before doing so, look in at the **Keramik-Museum** (▷ 26).

Dinner Public transport can take you all the way to Mitte at **Unter den Linden** (▷ 68). German dining should be on your agenda for the first day; **Palais Populaire** (▷ 72) is a good mid-range choice.

Evening For a classical performance, try the **Deutsche Oper Berlin** (▷ 27) or the **Konzerthaus** (▷ 71).

DAY 2

Morning Start out at the corner of **Friedrichstrasse** (▷ 61) and Kochstrasse to take in that relic from the Cold War, Checkpoint Charlie. Head up Friedrichstrasse, and pop into French-owned department store **Galeries Lafayette** (▷ 70) on the way. At Unter den Linden turn right. The **Staatsoper** (▷ 71) has a café that is open from 9am if you fancy a coffee or breakfast.

Mid-morning Cross the River Spree to **Museumsinsel** (▷ 78–79), thickly clustered with stellar museums.

Lunch You can go to one of the museum cafés for lunch; leave Museumsinsel and take in some American diner munchies on the far side of **Monbijoupark** (▷ 82), at **Sixties** (▷ 86).

Afternoon Stroll around some of the alternative galleries in and around the **Hackesche Höfe** (▷ 84, 85), before crossing Karl-Liebknecht-Strasse to the **Marx-Engels-Denkmal** memorial (▷ 82) to wonder what the founders of Communism would have made of it all.

Mid-afternoon Take some time to explore **Alexanderplatz** (▷ 76), the heart of the old East Berlin. Take the elevator to the top of the Fernsehturm for an unparalleled view over the city.

Dinner Take the U-Bahn two stops to Senefelderplatz and walk the short distance to **Kollwitzplatz** (▷ 93) and adjacent Wörther Strasse, to dine at the great Thai restaurant **Mao Thai Stammhaus** (▷ 96).

Evening Since you are now in trendy Prenzlauer Berg, why not take in some dance and music action at the **Kesselhaus** (▷ 95).

ESSENTIAL BERLIN TOP 25

▶ ▶ ▶

Alexanderplatz ▷ **76**
This historic square has
been transformed into a
bustling meeting place.

Bergmannkiez ▷ **52** This
major street encompasses
the multiethnic face of the
Kreuzberg district.

Berliner Dom ▷ **77** The
highly decorated dome of
Berlin's Protestant cathedral
is accessible to the public.

Zoo Berlin ▷ **34** One of
the world's most important
zoos, with outdoor enclo-
sures creating a sense of
openness.

Unter den Linden ▷ **68**
Fine buildings and superb
statues in the former heart
of imperial Berlin.

Topographie des Terrors
▷ **44** A memorial exhibition on the site of the former Gestapo headquarters.

Tiergarten ▷ **66–67**
A peaceful haven in the
heart of the city with ornamental gardens, lakes and
wooded areas to explore.

Spandauer Zitadelle
▷ **101** An attractive
suburb with an ancient
fortress on the rivers Havel
and Spree.

Schloss Charlottenburg
▷ **24–25** Explore this
lavish royal palace and its
riverside grounds, just minutes from central Berlin.

Reichstag ▷ **65** Visit the
spectacular glass dome of
the German parliament
building.

Pergamonmuseum ▷ **81**
Houses the city's impressive
collection of archaeological
discoveries.

Pariser Platz ▷ **64**
A handsome monumental
square that's at the heart
of Berlin.

These pages are a quick guide to the Top 25, which are described in more detail later. Here they are listed alphabetically and the tinted background shows which area they are in.

ESSENTIAL BERLIN TOP 25

Volkspark Humboldthain

PRENZLAUER BERG 87–94

Husemannstrasse

Gedenkstätte Berliner Mauer

Kollwitzplatz

Invaliden-park

UNTER DEN LINDEN 57–72

ALEXANDERPLATZ 73–86

Monbijou Park

Alexanderplatz

Pergamonmuseum

Museumsinsel

Berliner Dom

Reichstag

Unter den Linden

MITTE

NIKOLAIVIERTEL

Brandenburger Tor

Pariser Platz

Gendarmenmarkt

Tiergarten

Friedrichstrasse

Gemäldegalerie

Topographie des Terrors

POTSDAMER PLATZ 39–48

Oranienstrasse

KREUZBERG

KREUZBERG 49–56

Bergmannkiez

Viktoriapark

◀◀◀

9

Shopping

Berlin has plenty to offer shoppers, and the city is increasingly trading on its consumer appeal to attract visitors. You can buy everything here from designer labels and luxury jewelry to chic furniture and unusual gifts.

Retail Therapy

Brand shoppers and designer-label fans will be at home among names such as Gucci, Cerruti, Yamamoto and Diesel on Friedrichstrasse. Kurfürstendamm in the west of the city also has its fair share of the big names, including Versace and Chanel. There are more than a dozen department stores in the city catering to all tastes and trends. The opulent KaDeWe (Kaufhaus des Westens), just off Ku'damm, with a seemingly inexhaustible array of merchandise on six floors, is the largest. Galeries Lafayette, off Friedrichstrasse, has a fantastic food hall in the basement, and the Arkaden in Potsdamer Platz has a wide selection of top brands on three floors, with restaurants and cafés on the top floor for relaxing and refueling.

Individual Style

For something a little less mainstream you might want to head for the weird and wonderful shops around Oranienburger Strasse in Mitte, Bergmannstrasse and Oranienstrasse in Kreuzberg, and Goltzstrasse in Schöneberg for unusual shoes and bags, crazy clothes and sharp-looking shades and jewelry. Off the beaten track, spend an afternoon window-shopping or picking up one-off items in some of the offbeat shops around Kreuzberg and Prenzlauer Berg. Rosenthaler Strasse in Mitte is

Clockwise from top: stop at Confiserie Leysieffer for coffee and delectable chocolates; beer tankards make good

---

SECONDHAND

Trendsetters in this style-conscious capital are not afraid to celebrate the past. There are many retro and alternative clothing outlets around Prenzlauer Berg, but if you are serious about secondhand shopping head for the larger outlets such as Picknweight (Münzstrasse 19, Mitte), where you buy clothing by the kilo.

the heart of Berlin's alternative fashion scene, where you will find funky accessories, gifts and quirky up-and-coming designer boutiques. The city has a vibrant art scene, attracting dealers and collectors from all over the world; some of the most interesting art galleries are clustered around Auguststrasse in Mitte.

East and West

There are plenty of shops selling GDR memorabilia and clothing. A daily market in Alexanderplatz sells genuine army uniforms and badges; shops around Hackescher Markt and Prenzlauer Berg sell retro and cult clothing, accessories and souvenirs paying tribute to the city's history. Look out for souvenirs and clothing bearing the Ampelmann logo—the green-and-red-hat-wearing man seen at stop signs in the former east of the city. Other unique purchases include homemade chocolates, delicious breads and fine royal porcelain, both recent and antique items, made by KPM.

Malls

On days when the weather is simply too bad to be out on the street shopping, head for one of the big malls instead. For mainstream stores, the Europa-Center on Tauentzienstrasse, Bikini Berlin (Budapester Strasse), Mall of Berlin (Leipziger Platz), Alexa (Alexanderplatz), Friedrichstadt-Passagen (Friedrichstrasse) are all central.

souvenirs; puppets in a toy shop; sausages are a classic German food; military-style caps; Escada fashion store

ESSENTIAL BERLIN SHOPPING

MARKETS

Berlin has a huge number of flea markets selling clothing, jewelry and antiques. For surprising finds head for the antiques market (Wed–Mon) on Georgenstrasse under the S-Bahn arches. You can pick up some exotic bargains at the Turkish Market on Maybacher Ufer (Tuesday and Friday 11–6.30). Weekly street markets are a great place to experience the multicultural tastes of the city. The Winterfeldtplatz market on Wednesday and Saturday morning is the best. Mingle among the friendly crowd and sample Turkish, Italian and Greek delicacies.

Shopping by Theme

Whether you're looking for a department store, a quirky boutique, or something in between, you'll find it all in Berlin. On this page shops are listed by theme. For a more detailed write-up, see the individual listings in Berlin by Area.

Books
Antik- und Buchmarkt
  (▷ 70)
Dussmann (▷ 70)
Marga Schoeller
  Bücherstube (▷ 36)

**Clothes and
  Accessories**
BagAge (▷ 55)
Bleibgrün (▷ 36)
Chapeaux Hutmode
  Berlin (▷ 36)
Nix (▷ 85)
Tausche (▷ 95)

**Department Stores
  and Malls**
Friedrichstadt-Passagen
  (▷ 70)
Galeries Lafayette (▷ 70)
KaDeWe (Kaufhaus des
  Westens) (▷ 36)
Mall of Berlin (▷ 47)

Food and Drink
Berliner Kaffeerösterei
  (▷ 36)

Königsberger Marzipan
  Wald (▷ 27)
Rausch Schokoladenhaus
  (▷ 70)
Ritter Sport Bunte
  Schokowelt (▷ 70)

Galleries
Gipsformerei (▷ 27)
Hackesche Höfe (▷ 85)

Gifts and Souvenirs
Ampelmann (▷ 85)
Belladonna (▷ 55)
Berle's Trends and Gifts
  (▷ 70)
Berliner Zinnfiguren
  (▷ 36)
Erzgebirgskunst Original
  (▷ 85)
Harry Lehmann (▷ 27)
Haus am Checkpoint
  Charlie (▷ 70)
Museumsshop im
  Kulturforum (▷ 47)
RSVP Papier (▷ 85)
Sony Style Store (▷ 47)

The Home
Art & Industry (▷ 36)
Bella Casa (▷ 55)
Bürgelhaus (▷ 70)
Guru-Shop (▷ 93)
KPM (▷ 36)
Meissen Boutique
  (▷ 70)

Markets
Berliner Kunst Markt
  (▷ 70)
Trödelmarkt Strasse des
  17. Juni (▷ 36)
Türkischer Markt (▷ 55)
Winterfeldtplatz (▷ 36)

**Secondhand
  and Offbeat**
Da Capo (▷ 93)
Mr & Mrs Peppers
  (▷ 93)

Berlin by Night

After dark, Berlin buzzes with all kinds of entertainment. From opera and ballet to piano bars and jazz clubs, the city has something to offer every night owl. With virtually no restrictions on closing times, you can party into the small hours.

Cultural Mainstream

As a consequence of Berlin's former division into east and west it now boasts no fewer than three major orchestras and three opera companies, not to mention the Staatsballett. Berlin's numerous theaters cater to every taste, and many performances have English surtitles.

Musical Theater

For major shows like *Les Misérables*, check out the listings pages for venues such as Theater des Westens, Admiralspalast or Tipi Am Kanzleramt. The Friedrichstadtpalast, a revue theater with a vast stage where the shows are spectacular, is also popular with foreign visitors.

Bars and Clubs

Late-night entertainment tends to center on particular streets or neighborhoods. In Kreuzberg, that means Oranienstrasse or the Wrangelkiez; if you're in Mitte, then it's Hackescher Markt, Oranienburgerstrasse or the area between Torstrasse and Rosenthaler Platz. The KulturBrauerei on Schönhauser Allee is a good starting point in Prenzlauer Berg, as is Eberswalder Strasse. Charlottenburgers head for the Ku'damm or Savignyplatz.

LISTINGS

Useful listings magazines include *Prinz, Tip, Zitty* (all twice-monthly, in German); *Berlin Das Magazin* (quarterly, in English and German); *Berlin Programm* (monthly, in German). *Prinz* also publishes an annual magazine picking out the best restaurants, shops, bars, clubs and hotels. Berlin Tourismus Marketing publishes *Berlin-Kalendar* every two months in English and German. Online, berlinatnight.de is informative.

By night Berlin is an illuminated wonder of modern and Romanesque architecture

Where to Eat

Sure, Berlin is a great place for trying regional German cuisine. But increasing cosmopolitanism, wealth and confidence has spawned a wave of new and varied dining experiences to suit all palates. At the cutting edge are the 21 restaurants currently boasting Michelin stars.

International

Indian or Thai, Australian or Lebanese—the choice seems unending. The Italian community has been running restaurants in Charlottenburg since the 1960s, while Berlin's large Turkish community centers on Kreuzberg, where inexpensive meals are served in dozens of small restaurants and at *Imbiss* (fast food) stands. In Mitte, commercial artists rub shoulders with diners in the renovated courtyards (*Höfe*) around Hackescher Markt and Oranienburger Strasse. The menus here feature everything from Spanish tapas and American ribs to Asian fusion. Gentrified Prenzlauer Berg also has a thriving eating-out culture—start looking in Schönhauser Allee or Kollwitzplatz. Berlin is also great for vegetarians and vegans, with more than 50 restaurants in the city.

German Cuisine

Berlin home cooking (a specialty of many pubs, old and new), while nourishing, is heavily meat based and high in calories. You may prefer the more imaginative, though pricier, "new German cuisine" (*neue Deutsche Küche*). Look also for German restaurants and pubs serving craft beer with meals, some of it locally produced.

SMOKING BAN

Smoking is banned inside restaurants, bars, pubs and clubs, and anyone breaking the law faces a fine. There was some resistance to the ban in Berlin, so an exception was made for some traditional pubs (*Kneipen*), providing that no cooked food was prepared on the premises. Such pubs are usually designated *Raucherkneipen* or *Raucherlokale*. Elsewhere, smoking is usally permitted on terraces.

From street cafés to sophisticated restaurants, Berlin offers a plethora of dining experiences

Where to Eat by Cuisine

There are places to eat to suit all tastes and budgets in Berlin. On this page they are listed by cuisine. For a more detailed description of each venue, see Berlin by Area.

American
Sixties (▷ 86)

Asian
Amrit (▷ 56)
Good Friends (▷ 28)
Mao Thai Stammhaus (▷ 96)
Monsieur Vuong (▷ 86)
Tokyohaus (▷ 28)

Australian
Corroboree (▷ 48)

Austrian
Diener Tattersaal (▷ 38)

Breweries
Brauhaus Lemke (▷ 28)
Doldem Mädel (▷ 56)
Lindenbräu (▷ 48)

Cafés
Café am Engelbecken (▷ 56)
Café Einstein (▷ 72)
Café Einstein Stammhaus (▷ 48)
Caffè e Gelato (▷ 48)
LePopulaire (▷ 72)
Soupkultur (▷ 38)
Zum Nussbaum (▷ 86)

German, Traditional
Bergmann Curry (▷ 56)
Henne (▷ 56)
Kaisersaal (▷ 48)
Kartoffelkiste (▷ 38)
Knese (▷ 38)
Konnopke's Imbiss (▷ 96)
Marjellchen (▷ 38)
Metzer Eck (▷ 96)
Nante Eck (▷ 72)
Prater Garten (▷ 96)
Restaurant Schlossgarten (▷ 28)

German, Modern
Acht&Dreissig (▷ 86)
Neugrüns Köche (▷ 96)
PeterPaul (▷ 96)
Schnitzelei (▷ 28)

European
Borchardt (▷ 72)
Facil (▷ 48)
Frannz (▷ 96)
Funkturm Restaurant (▷ 28)
Galija am Schloss (▷ 28)
Hackescher Hof (▷ 86)
Hugos (▷ 38)
Lokal (▷ 86)

Lutter & Wegner (▷ 38, 72)
Taverna Athene (▷ 56)
Wintergarten im Literaturhaus (▷ 38)

Italian
Bocca di Bacco (▷ 72)
Oxymoron (▷ 86)
Trattoria Piazza Rossa (▷ 86)

Pacific
Vox (▷ 48)

Russian
Pasternak (▷ 96)

Turkish
Hasir (▷ 56)
Istanbul (▷ 28)

Vegetarian
Cookies Cream (▷ 72)

Top Tips For...

These great suggestions will help you tailor your ideal visit to Berlin, no matter how you choose to spend your time. Each sight or listing has a fuller write-up elsewhere in the book.

CHIC SHOPPING

Bleibgrün (▷ 36): Dress yourself in the latest international fashions at this cutting-edge store.
Galeries Lafayette (▷ 70): Shop until you drop while admiring Jean Nouvel's magnificent architecture.
KaDeWe (▷ 36): Europe's biggest upmarket department store after Harrods also boasts a world-famous food hall.
Rausch Schokoladenhaus (▷ 70): Submit to temptation in this luxurious emporium overlooking beautiful Gendarmenmarkt. Chocolate replicas of the Brandenburg Gate a specialty.

HOME COOKING

Lokal (▷ 86): Sample the much talked-about "New German Cuisine"—and the freshest local produce—in a cozy, faux-rustic setting.
Henne (▷ 56): Anything you want, so long as it's roast chicken.
Brauhaus Lemke (▷ 28): Look no further than this craft beer temple if you relish tasty Berlin cooking, home-brewed ales and stunning views of Schloss Charlottenburg.
Marjellchen (▷ 38): Road test dishes based on traditional East Prussian recipes.
Prater Garten (▷ 96): While away a summer's afternoon in what's reckoned to be Berlin's oldest beer garden (1837).

VIEW FROM ABOVE

Bundestag (▷ 65): View Sir Norman Foster's spectacular glass dome from the inside before watching German politicians at work below.
Fernsehturm (▷ 76): Dine out in the TV tower's famous revolving restaurant.
Siegessäule (▷ 66): Climb to the top of the Victory Column for panoramic views of the city.

Clockwise from top: Zoo Berlin; take in some blues at one of the city's jazz clubs; modern mosaic in the Hotel Transit

ESSENTIAL BERLIN   TOP TIPS FOR...

Berlin Hi-Flyer (▷ 69): Take a day or night ride in a high-flying helium balloon, tethered 150m above Mitte.

HOT AND COOL
A-Trane Jazz Club (▷ 37): Reserve a seat on the A-train, then sit back and enjoy the ride into the contemporary jazz scene. The Saturday night jam sessions are the stuff of legends.
Kesselhaus (▷ 95): Join the night owls and dance the night away in a former brewery.
Strandbar Mitte (▷ 82): Enjoy a cocktail under the palm trees at this popular Monbijou Park beach bar overlooking Museums Island.
Zoo Berlin (▷ 34): Escape the summer heat by heading to the Penguin House, where the temperatures can drop to near freezing point.

A BIT OF CULTURE
Berliner Ensemble (▷ 71): Sit back and enjoy Bertolt Brecht's *Threepenny Opera* in the setting for which it was created.
Gemäldegalerie (▷ 42): See Rembrandt's masterpiece *Susanna and the Elders*, among others, in this world-class art museum.
Philharmonie (▷ 47): Plan ahead to get hold of a highly prized ticket to a concert by the renowned Berlin Philharmonic orchestra. There are also free chamber concerts in the foyer (Tue 1pm).
Staatsoper Unter den Linden (▷ 71): Enjoy world-class opera under the baton of music director Daniel Barenboim in a restored 18th-century concert hall.

GOING FOR A SONG
Schloss Charlottenburg (▷ 24): There's no entry fee to stroll in the grounds and admire the wonderful architecture at your leisure.
Mauerpark (▷ 92): Round off your Sunday visit to the Berlin Wall by joining in the Sunday evening karaoke concert.
Trödelmarkt Strasse des 17. Juni (▷ 36): Have a rummage and you might just pick up that valuable antique for a song.

Loft in Prenzlauer Berg; Berlin Hi-Flyer, a tethered helium balloon; café culture is thriving in this vibrant city

Wannsee-Kladow ferry (▷ 104): Cross
Wannsee and the River Havel to scenic Kladow,
taking in two islands en route, for no more than
the cost of a BVG ticket.

ACTIVITIES FOR KIDS
Filmpark Babelsberg (▷ 102): Go behind the
scenes at a movie studio.
Sea Life Berlin (▷ 83): Dive into the depths of
the underwater world.
Zeiss-Grossplanetarium (▷ 104): See the
stars in their eyes.
Zoo Berlin (▷ 34): Visit the zoo and aquarium
here.

WORLD WAR II SITES
Brandenburger Tor (▷ 60): See where the
Nazis held triumphal military processions.
Gedenkstätte Deutscher Widerstand (▷ 45):
Visit the headquarters of the army officers who
led the failed 1944 July Plot against Hitler.
Denkmal für die Ermordeten Juden Europas
(▷ 69): Contemplate the monument to the six
million Jewish victims of the Nazi terror.
Kaiser-Wilhelm-Gedächtniskirche (▷ 32):
Pause for a moment to remember the victims
of war at this bombed-out memorial church.

REVISITING THE COLD WAR
Checkpoint Charlie (▷ 61, 70): Stop for a
selfie at the former border crossing, where US
and Soviet Russian tanks once engaged in a
deadly stand-off.
Gedenkstätte Berliner Mauer (▷ 90): Survey
the former death strip of the Berlin Wall from a
viewing tower and discover the personal stories
of people who risked their lives trying to cross it.
Glienicker Brücke (▷ 106): Cross the
bridge over the River Havel where spies were
exchanged in the 1960s, then see the 2015
movie *Bridge of Spies* (filmed here) when you
get home.
Rathaus Schöneberg: Stand in the spot where
President Kennedy famously declared: "Ich bin
ein Berliner."

*From top: Grossplanetarium;
Brandenburger Tor; Cold War
signs at Checkpoint Charlie;
Glienicker Bridge*

The leafy, western district of Charlottenburg is immersed in its own pursuit of the good life, with opulent Schloss Charlottenburg the most obvious stellar attraction of a quarter that is wealthy and self-assured.

Top 25

0
250 m

0
250 yds

C D E

Schloss Charlottenburg

HIGHLIGHTS

- White Hall
- Golden Gallery
- Gobelins' tapestry rooms
- Study and bedchamber of Friedrich I
- *Embarkation for Cythera*, J. A. Watteau
- Silver Vault
- Porcelain Cabinet
- Schinkel Pavillon
- Great Orangery
- Gardens

TIP

- Try to make time to join the guided tour (extra cost) of the opulent private apartments of King Friedrich I and Electress Sophie Charlotte.

This attractive former royal palace, built in the rococo style, lies only a stone's throw from the heart of Berlin. The Schloss was built over more than 100 years, its development mirroring the rise of the ruling Hohenzollern dynasty.

Royal retreat The Electress Sophie Charlotte's rural retreat—this suburb of Berlin was still deep in the countryside and considered suitable for a summer palace—was designed by Johann Arnold Nering in 1695. It was transformed into the palace you see today during the reigns of Friedrich I and Friedrich II by the architect von Knobelsdorff, who added the Neuer Flügel (New Wing). Here you can see the staterooms and the glorious Golden Gallery and White Hall ballrooms. The Great Orangery and Theater

Clockwise from far left: this restored Prussian palace was built as a summer retreat for Queen Sophie Charlotte; decoration on the palace entrance gates; the Galerie der Romantik on the ground floor has 19th-century works, including Arcadian Landscape (1805) by Philipp Hackert; Heinrike Dannecker (1802) by Gottlieb Schick

form wings of the palace, along with the Langhans Building at the western end of the Orangery. Dominating the forecourt is Andreas Schlüter's superb equestrian statue of the Great Elector, Friedrich Wilhelm, father of Friedrich I.

Riverside grounds Do not leave Schloss Charlottenburg without exploring the delightful grounds, which slope towards the River Spree. The formal French garden is a marked contrast to the landscaped English garden, which houses the Mausoleum built for Queen Luise, and the Belvedere, now a museum devoted to Berlin porcelain. Closer to the palace is the delightfully idiosyncratic Neue Pavillon, designed by Berlin's best-known 19th-century architect, Karl Friedrich Schinkel. Today the palace gardens are a popular public park.

THE BASICS

spsg.de

✚ A4

✉ Spandauer Damm

☎ 030 32 09 10

🕐 Altes Schloss: Apr–Oct Tue–Sun 10–5.30; Nov–Mar 10–4.30. Neuer Flügel: Apr–Oct Tue–Sun 10–5.30; Nov–Mar 10–4.30

🍴 Restaurant

Ⓤ U-Bahn Richard-Wagner-Platz, Sophie-Charlotte-Platz

🚌 M45, 109, 309

💶 Expensive

More to See

BRÖHAN-MUSEUM
broehan-museum.de

In 1983, Professor Karl H. Bröhan presented his superb collection of Jugendstil (art nouveau), art deco and functionalist crafts to the city. The highlights of the museum are beautifully decorated rooms in the styles of the leading designers of the period. The porcelain collection is particularly fine.

➕ A5 ✉ Schlossstrasse 1a ☎ 030 32 69 06 00 🕐 Tue–Sun 10–6 🚇 U-Bahn Sophie-Charlotte-Platz, Richard-Wagner-Platz 🚌 M45, 109, 309 💷 Moderate

FUNKTURM
funkturm-messeberlin.de

Berlin's broadcasting tower was built between 1924 and 1926. It reaches up 150m (492ft) above the Messegelände Congress Center, and has a restaurant (▷ 28) at 55m (180ft), and a viewing platform at 126m (413ft).

➕ Off map A6 ✉ Hammarskjöldplatz, Messedamm 22 ☎ 030 30 38 19 05 🕐 Mon 10–8, Tue–Sun 10am–11pm

🚈 S-Bahn Messe Nord/ICC 🚌 M49, X34, 104, 139, 218 💷 Moderate

KERAMIK-MUSEUM BERLIN
keramik-museum-berlin.de

Tucked away in a 1712 town house not far from Schloss Charlottenburg, the Ceramic Museum is something of a labor of love. The permanent collection ranges from the mid-19th century to the modern day, enhanced by temporary exhibitions.

➕ B5 ✉ Schustehrusstrasse 13 ☎ 030 32 12 322 🕐 Fri–Mon 1–5 🚇 U-Bahn Richard-Wagner-Platz 💷 Inexpensive

MUSEUM BERGGRUEN
smb.museum

Heinz Berggruen's art collection focuses on paintings and sculptures by Picasso and his contemporaries, including Klee, Matisse, Braque and Giacometti. The Picassos span the artist's entire career.

➕ A5 ✉ Schlossstrasse 1 ☎ 030 266 42 42 42 🕐 Tue–Fri 10–6, Sat–Sun 11-6 🚇 U-Bahn Sophie-Charlotte-Platz 💷 Moderate

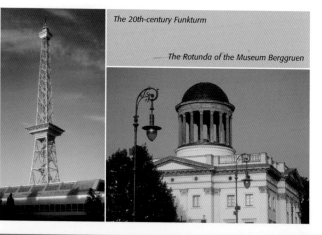

The 20th-century Funkturm

The Rotunda of the Museum Berggruen

Shopping

GIPSFORMEREI
smb-webshop.de
This is the place to come for top-quality plaster reproductions of famous items from Berlin's museums, such as a bust of Queen Nefertiti.
🗺 Off map ✉ Sophie-Charlotten-Strasse 17–18 ☎ 030 326 76 90 🚇 S-Bahn Westend

HARRY LEHMANN
parfum-individual.de
In business since 1926, this family-owned shop creates and sells good,
moderately priced, non-designer perfumes from secret recipes.
🗺 B6 ✉ Kantstrasse 106 ☎ 030 324 35 82
🚇 U-Bahn Wilmersdorfer Strasse

KÖNIGSBERGER MARZIPAN WALD
wald-koenigsberger-marzipan.com
This long-running, family confectioners is the place to come for traditional Königsberger marzipan.
🗺 A6 ✉ Pestalozzistrasse 54a ☎ 030 323 82 54 🚇 U-Bahn Sophie-Charlotte-Platz

Entertainment and Nightlife

BLACKLIST BAR
blacklist-bar.de
Enjoy a classy cocktail here or take to the small dance floor. Music is provided by the resident DJ.
🗺 A6 ✉ Neue Kantstrasse 1 ☎ 01522 93 42 614 🚇 U-Bahn Sophie-Charlotte-Platz

CAFÉ THEATER SCHALOTTE
schalotte.de
This one-time movie theater has been artfully transformed into a venue for alternative theater, cabaret and music.
🗺 B5 ✉ Behaimstrasse 22 ☎ 030 341 14 85 🚇 U-Bahn Richard-Wagner-Platz

DEUTSCHE OPER BERLIN
deutscheoperberlin.de
The German Opera has been staging opera and ballet, and classical concerts since 1912. Performances are held in Fritz Bornemann's contemporary glass-fronted building. Even the less expensive seats provide a great view and acoustics are superb.

🗺 B6 ✉ Bismarckstrasse 35 ☎ 030 343 84 01; tickets 030 343 84 343 🕐 Mon–Sat 11–1 and 1 hour before performance, Sun 10–2 and 1 hour before performance 🚇 U-Bahn Deutsche Oper

WILHELM HOECK
wilhelm-hoeck.de
Settle down to enjoy a glass of foaming pilsner beer amid the venerable surroundings of this neighborhood *Kneipe* that's been a popular watering hole and Charlottenburg institution since 1892.
🗺 B6 ✉ Wilmersdorfer Strasse 149 ☎ 030 34 50 98 48 🚇 U-Bahn Bismarckstrasse

---

LOCAL BARS

Tradition-conscious Berliners feel most at home in their friendly local *Kneipe* (pub). Most of these are not much frequented by tourists, since smoking is often permitted and meals may not be cooked on site. One notable exception is Wilhem Hoeck, which is now smoke-free.

Where to Eat

Prices are approximate, based on a
3-course meal for one person.

€€€ over €40
€€ €20–€40
€ under €20

BRAUHAUS LEMKE (€€)

lemke.berlin
Traditional fare such as Berlin liver
(*Leber*), knuckle of pork (*Eisbein*) and of
course *Currywurst* is served with modern
craft beer from the Lemke brewery, along
with guest ales.
🔲 B4 ✉ Luisenplatz 1 ☎ 030 341 93
88 🕐 Sun–Thu 9am–1am, Fri–Sat 9am–2am
🚇 U-Bahn Richard-Wagner-Platz

FUNKTURM RESTAURANT (€€)

funkturm-messeberlin.de
From 55m (180ft) up on the Radio
Tower (▷ 26), the view outside is
matched by 1920s-style decor inside.
There is a themed buffet in the evening.
🔲 Off map, west of A6 ✉ Messedamm 22
☎ 030 30 38 29 00 🕐 Tue 6pm–11pm, Wed–
Sun 11.30–11 🚇 S-Bahn Messe Nord/ICC

GALIJA AM SCHLOSS (€€)

galija-am-schloss.de
A Charlottenburg institution, this lively
Croatian-German restaurant serves
grilled meat in large portions, as well as
fish dishes.
🔲 C5 ✉ Otto-Suhr-Allee 139 ☎ 030 341 70
41 🕐 Daily 11.30–11.30 🚇 U-Bahn Richard-
Wagner-Platz

GOOD FRIENDS (€€)

goodfriends-berlin.de
This is the place to go in Charlottenburg
for delicious Cantonese cooking.
🔲 C6 ✉ Kantstrasse 30 ☎ 030 313 26 59
🕐 Daily 12pm–1am 🚇 S-Bahn Savignyplatz

ISTANBUL (€€)

istanbul-restaurant-berlin.de
Considered by many locals to be the
finest Turkish eatery in town, the
Istanbul offers authentic Turkish cuisine,
including kebabs, meze and desserts,
and the service is friendly.
🔲 B6 ✉ Pestalozzistrasse 84 ☎ 030 883
27 77 🕐 Daily 10am–midnight 🚇 U-Bahn
Wilmersdorfer Strasse

RESTAURANT SCHLOSSGARTEN (€€)

restaurant-schlossgarten-berlin.de
Traditional German fish and meat
dishes are served in this popular
restaurant and there's a special venison
menu, a reminder that the area was
formerly the hunting grounds of
Charlottenburg palace.
🔲 C5 ✉ Schlossstrasse 64 ☎ 030 36 70
22 99 🕐 Mon–Sat 11.30–10, Sun 11.30–8
🚇 U-Bahn Richard-Wagner-Platz

SCHNITZELEI (€€)

schnitzelei.de
The natural wood decor here is a
perfect match for the Alpine cuisine.
Dishes are served tapas-style, and there
are (despite the name) vegetarian and
vegan options.
🔲 C5 ✉ Röntgenstrasse 7 ☎ 030 34 70 27
78 ☎ Mon–Fri 4pm–midnight, Sat–Sun 12–12
🚇 U-Bahn Richard-Wagner-Platz

TOKYOHAUS (€€)

tokyohaus.de
Sushi and teppanyaki are both freshly
prepared and served at this Japanese
restaurant that doesn't allow its love
of showmanship to get in the way of
traditional craft.
🔲 B8 ✉ Brandenburgischche Strasse 30
☎ 01768 43 33 446 ☎ Mon–Thu 4–11,
Fri–Sun 12–11 🚇 U-Bahn Adenauerplatz

Around Kurfürstendamm

The great boulevard Kurfürstendamm is known locally as the "Ku'damm." There's far more to the bustling Ku'damm district than its renowned thoroughfare, however, as a stroll around its busy neighboring streets will confirm.

Top 25

DES 17 JUNI

Tiergarten

Neuer
See

Landwehrkanal

Drakestr

Rauchstrasse

Corneliusstrasse

Kath.-Heinroth-Ufer

Zoo Berlin

Aquarium

BUDAPESTER   STRASSE

P

KURFÜRSTENSTRASSE

Burggrafenstr

STRASSE

STRASSE

Passauer Strasse

Ansbacher strasse

Around Kurfürstendamm

E   F   G

Kaiser-Wilhelm-Gedächtniskirche

TOP 25

The bomb-damaged original church now stands as a war memorial

HIGHLIGHTS

- Cross of nails
- Surviving mosaics
- The Stalingrad Madonna
- Bell tower
- Globe Fountain

TIP

- There are regular guided tours of the church lasting around 30 minutes. For details, tel 01731 14 08 044. Tours are free in German and €5 in English.

This blackened ruin of a church, heavily damaged by Allied bombing raids in 1943, stands as a reminder of the horrors of war. Particularly moving is the cross of nails given by the people of Coventry, in England, another war-torn city.

War memorial The Gedächtniskirche, built in 1895 in Romanesque style, was Kaiser Wilhelm II's contribution to the developing New West End. No expense was spared on the interior, and the dazzling mosaics are deliberately reminiscent of St. Mark's in Venice. After Allied bombs destroyed the church in 1943, the shell was allowed to stand, though the tower and clock were given a facelift in 2015. Poignantly, the old building now serves as a small museum focusing on the wartime destruction.

The New Chapel Berliners have denigrated the uncompromisingly modern octagonal chapel and hexagonal stained-glass tower. However, many visitors find peace in the blue-hued chapel, whose stained glass is from Chartres, France. The chapel was designed by Egon Eiermann in the early 1960s.

Breitscheidplatz The area around the church has been transformed in recent years, with the addition of the high-rise Waldorf-Astoria Hotel and its viewing window (Zoofenster) over the Zoo and Tiergarten. Nearby is Germany's first concept mall, Bikini Berlin, which eschews the big chains in favor of local start-up companies.

Kurfürstendamm

The "Ku'damm" is the place for the latest fashions as well as chic modern art

It would be unthinkable to come to Berlin without visiting the "Ku'damm," the majestic tree-lined boulevard that runs west through Charlottenburg for 3.5km (2 miles) and its flagship stores, cafés, restaurants, theaters and cinemas.

Showcase Charlottenburg became the center of West Berlin when the city was partitioned after World War II, and Kufürstendamm evolved into its main shopping street, with luxurious hotels and department stores springing up along its length. Many of these were refurbished during the boom years of the 1960s.

New West End The elegant streets off the Ku'damm—Fasanenstrasse, for example—were part of the New West End, which was developed as a residential area at the end of the 19th century. Some of the houses here are now art galleries; at Fasanenstrasse 24 is a museum devoted to the 20th-century artist Käthe Kollwitz. Next door is the Literaturhaus, a cultural hub with a garden café (▷ 38). Villa Grisebach at No. 25 is an outstanding example of Jugendstil architecture. On the corner of Leibnizstrasse is another period piece, the Iduna House, whose cupola dates from 1907.

Savignyplatz This square was laid out as a garden in the 1920s. Nowadays its restaurants and shaded sidewalk cafés cluster as far as the railway arches. Also nearby is the Theater des Westens (▷ 37).

(▷ 38) (▷ 37)

THE BASICS

➕ D7
🚇 U-Bahn Kurfürstendamm; U-Bahn Uhlandstrasse
🚌 X10, M19, M29, 109, 110
🚉 Zoologischer Garten

Literaturhaus and Wintergarten Café
literaturhaus-berlin.de
➕ D7
✉ Fasanenstrasse 23
☎ 030 887 28 60
🕐 Mon–Fri 10–5; café daily 9am–midnight
🍴 Excellent
♿ Free

Käthe-Kollwitz-Museum
kaethe-kollwitz.de
➕ D7
✉ Fasanenstrasse 24
☎ 030 882 52 10
🕐 Daily 11–6
♿ Moderate

HIGHLIGHTS

● Literaturhaus
● Käthe-Kollwitz-Museum
● Fasanenstrasse
● Iduna House
● The KaDeWe department store
● Neoclassical newsstands

Zoo Berlin

Elephants exchanging a greeting at the zoo (left); the giraffe enclosure (right)

THE BASICS

zoo-berlin.de

Zoo

✚ E6

✉ Hardenbergplatz 8

☎ 030 25 40 10

🕐 Daily 9–7 (closes earlier out of season)

🚇 U- or S-Bahn Zoologischer Garten

✋ Expensive. Joint ticket with Aquarium available

Aquarium

aquarium-berlin.de

✚ E7

✉ Budapester Strasse 32

☎ 030 25 40 10

🕐 Daily 9–6

✋ Expensive. Joint ticket with Zoo available

HIGHLIGHTS

● Bao Bao, the giant panda
● Feeding polar bears and seals
● Hippopotamus House
● Baby elephant enclosure
● Komodo dragons

Berlin's zoo has developed into one of the most important in the world, with more than 20,000 animals and 1,500 species represented.

The King of Prussia The zoo dates back to 1841, when Friedrich Wilhelm IV donated his pheasant gardens and exotic animal collection to the citizens of Berlin. After the zoo suffered serious damage during World War II, the director, Dr. Katharina Heinroth, began the lengthy process of rebuilding it.

The Zoo At Germany's oldest and best-known zoo, moats and trenches rather than bars and cages define the outdoor enclosures, creating a sense of openness and giving visitors a clear view of the animals. In the Hippopotamus House, glass domes cover the steamy, climate-controlled home of the common and pygmy hippopotamuses. A glass wall in the viewing gallery allows you to watch them swimming under water. The polar bears and seals are also free to swim around in their homes; the seals even have their own wave machine.

The Aquarium A huge statue of an iguanodon, which became extinct 90 million years ago, guards the entrance here. The aquarium is home to a variety of fish, frogs, lizards, snakes, crocodiles and turtles from all over the world. The Komodo dragons dominate the reptile area on the second floor. Measuring 3m (10ft) in length, they are the largest lizards in the world.

A Walk around Kurfürstendamm

Kurfürstendamm, or "Ku'damm," is Berlin's most famous shopping area. This walk also takes in the zoo.

DISTANCE: 3.5km (2.2 miles) **ALLOW:** 1.5 hours

START

WITTENBERGPLATZ U-BAHN STATION
E7 U-Bahn Wittenbergplatz

END

ZOOLOGISCHER GARTEN STATION
D6 Zoologischer Garten

1 Head west down Tauentzien-strasse, then turn right into Nürn-berger Strasse and walk down to the zoo. Enter through the Elephant Gate at Budapester Strasse 34.

2 Stroll through the zoo to emerge at Hardenbergplatz. Turn left, keeping Zoo Station on your right. Cross over the intersection and turn right to walk up Hardenbergstrasse.

3 Turn left onto Fasanenstrasse. The Ludwig-Ehrhardt-Haus (No. 85, home of the Chamber of Commerce) on your left is one of the most interesting modern buildings in this part of the city.

4 Cross over Fasanenstrasse. On your left you'll come to the Jewish center at No. 79. It was built in 1959 on the site of the synagogue, destroyed by the Nazis in 1938.

8 At the corner of Uhlandstrasse you'll find the massive homeware design store Stilwerk. Continue down Kantstrasse, then turn left onto Joachimstaler Strasse to Zoologischer Garten station.

7 Pass the legendary bars and bistros around Savignyplatz to Kantstrasse and turn right.

6 Retrace your steps to Ku'damm and turn left. Stroll slowly along Berlin's most famous boulevard to Knesebeckstrasse, where you turn right. Head down to Savignyplatz, the setting of the movie *Cabaret*.

5 Continue south. The magnificent buildings south of Ku'damm are reminiscent of the imperial era, and now contain the most elegant shops in town. At No. 23 is the Literaturhaus, which has a wonderful café.

Shopping

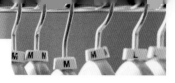

ART & INDUSTRY
aiberlin.de
Shop here for furniture, lamps and accessories in Bauhaus and other functionalist styles, as well as watches.

⊞ C7 ✉ Bleibtreustrasse 40 ☎ 030 883 49 46 🚇 S-Bahn Savignyplatz

BERLINER KAFFEERÖSTEREI
berliner-kaffeeroesterei.de
A mixed aroma of roasting coffee beans, tea, cocoa and pralines emanates from this old-fashioned shop.

⊞ D7 ✉ Uhlandstrasse 173–174 ☎ 030 88 67 79 20 🚇 U-Bahn Uhlandstrasse

BERLINER ZINNFIGUREN
zinnfigur.com
A small piece of Prussian military tradition survives here, in hand-painted pewter figurines of soldiers from ancient times to the 19th century.

⊞ D6 ✉ Knesebeckstrasse 88 ☎ 030 315 70 00 🚇 S-Bahn Savignyplatz

BLEIBGRÜN
bleibgruen.de
Cutting-edge designer fashions and shoes straight off the Paris catwalk are the stock-in-trade here.

⊞ C7 ✉ Bleibtreustrasse 29 ☎ 030 882 16 89 🚇 S-Bahn Savignyplatz

CHAPEAUX-HUTMODE BERLIN
chapeaux-hutmode-berlin.de
Ladies' hats of all kinds are on sale here, from retro to frivolous to razor-sharp contemporary.

⊞ C6 ✉ Bleibtreustrasse 51 ☎ 030 312 09 13 🚇 S-Bahn Savignyplatz

KADEWE
kadewe.de
Kaufhaus des Westens is the largest department store in continental Europe The focus is on luxury, so it can be pricey. The top two floors are devoted to food, with a gourmet Food Hall and a top-floor café with fantastic views over Wittenbergplatz.

⊞ E7 ✉ Tauentzienstrasse 21–24 ☎ 030 212 10 🚇 U-Bahn Wittenbergplatz

KPM
kpm-berlin.com
Quality porcelain bearing the Königliche Porzellan-Manufaktur hallmark is on sale here, but many visitors come just to tour the factory and learn about the art and skills on display.

⊞ E5 ✉ Wegelystrasse 1 ☎ 030 39 00 90 🚇 S-Bahn Tiergarten

MARGA SCHOELLER BÜCHERSTUBE
margaschoeller.de
This long-established bookstore has a large English-language section, including magazines about Berlin.

⊞ D7 ✉ Knesebeckstrasse 33 ☎ 030 881 11 12 🚇 S-Bahn Savignyplatz

TRÖDELMARKT STRASSE DES 17. JUNI
berlinertroedelmarkt.com
Berlin's oldest and largest flea market is great for retro bargains and antiques.

⊞ D5–E5 ✉ Tiergarten ☎ 030 26 55 00 96 🕐 Sat–Sun 10–5 🚇 U-Bahn Ernst-Reuter-Platz

WINTERFELDTPLATZ
A pleasant way to spend a Saturday morning is to explore the antiques shops around Motzstrasse, before homing in on one of Berlin's most vibrant street markets, in Winterfeldtplatz. You never know quite what you will find here—everything from hand-me-down jewelry to flowers to pretty children's clothes.

A-TRANE JAZZ CLUB

a-trane.de

This lively buzzing Charlottenburg night haunt caters to lovers of modern jazz and bebop.

🚹 C6 ✉ Bleibtreustrasse 1 ☎ 030 313 25 50 🚇 S-Bahn Savignyplatz 🚌 X34, M49

CAFÉ KEESE

cafekeese-berlin.de

Something of a Berlin institution, this rather formal dance hall, which has been going strong since the 1960s, caters more to an older crowd.

🚹 C6 ✉ Bismarckstrasse 108 ☎ 030 312 91 11 🚇 U-Bahn Ernst-Reuter-Platz

JOURNEY INTO THE NIGHT

journeyintothenight.com

New on the scene is this small and cozy cocktail bar hidden in the railway arches near Savignyplatz. The DJ entertains in the small hours.

🚹 D6 ✉ Else-Ury-Bogen 605 ☎ 0172 666 63 37 🚇 S-Bahn Savignyplatz

MOMMSEN-ECK

mommsen-eck.de

This traditional wood-rich pub with a friendly atmosphere has been serving German food and more than 100 types of beer for over a century.

🚹 C7 ✉ Mommsenstrasse 45 ☎ 030 324 25 80 🚇 S-Bahn Charlottenburg

MONKEY BAR

monkeybarberlin.de

A new kid on the block, Monkey Bar is named for its terrace views of Berlin Zoo. Inside, DJs host the party; you can join the crowd on the small dance floor or just listen to the music.

🚹 E7 ✉ Hotel 25hours Bikini (10th floor), Budapester Strasse 40 ☎ 030 120 23 12 10 🚇 U- or S-Bahn Zoologischer Garten

MONSIEUR BOURGOGNE

wine-bar-cellar-monsieur-bourgogne.business.site

This small wine shop and bar is a good place to linger over tastings of Burgundy wine or the fine pork, poultry and cheese platters from the same region.

🚹 D6 ✉ Carmerstrasse 11 ☎ 0174 820 32 78 🚇 S-Bahn Savignyplatz

QUASIMODO

quasimodo.de

Stifling and crowded, this cellar bar is a good place to hear live jazz, blues and funk.

🚹 D7 ✉ Kantstrasse 12a ☎ 030 31 80 45 60 🚇 U- or S-Bahn Zoologischer Garten

THEATER DES WESTENS

stage-entertainment.de

A graceful theater dating from 1896 is the place to go for big-budget spectacles and translations of Broadway and West End musicals.

🚹 D7 ✉ Kantstrasse 12 ☎ 030 31 90 30 🚇 U- and S-Bahn Zoologischer Garten

TIMES BAR

hotel-savoy.com

Named after the clocks showing world times that decorate the wall, this is a cozy place to settle down to read.

🚹 D7 ✉ Savoy Hotel, Fasanenstrasse 9–10 ☎ 030 31 10 33 36 🚇 U-Bahn Uhlandstrasse

VAN GOGH

van-gogh.de

This cozy piano bar has been a hit with Berliners from the get-go, more than 20 years ago. Sip a cocktail, soak up the atmosphere and wallow in the music: classical, jazz, pop—whatever takes the keyboard player's fancy.

🚹 D7 ✉ Grolmanstrasse 41/3 ☎ 030 88 42 68 09 🚇 S-Bahn Savignyplatz

Where to Eat

PRICES

Prices are approximate, based on a
3-course meal for one person.

€€€ over €40
€€   €20–€40
€   up to €20

DIENER TATTERSALL (€€)

diener-berlin.de

You are guaranteed to get a warm
welcome at this homey old-style pub
serving top-notch Austrian cuisine,
washed down with Berlin beer.

🔟 D7 ✉ Grolmanstrasse 47 ☎ 030
881 53 29 🕐 Daily 6pm–3am 🚇 S-Bahn
Savignyplatz

HUGOS (€€€)

hugos-restaurant.de

Chef Eberhard Lange has a Michelin star
for his Mediterranean-inspired haute cuisine. The restaurant is on the top floor
of the Hotel InterContinental so you can
enjoy the splendid views as you dine.

🔟 F6 ✉ Budapester Strasse 2 ☎ 030 26 02
12 63 🕐 Tue–Sat 6.30pm–10.30 🚇 U- and
S-Bahn Zoologischer Garten

KARTOFFELKISTE (€€)

kartoffelkiste.de

Tuck into wholesome and hearty
German cooking at this restaurant dedicated to the humble potato. Every dish
contains potato in some shape or form,
and that includes the pizza bases.

🔟 E7 ✉ Europa-Center, 1 Etage,
Breitscheidplatz ☎ 030 261 42 54 🕐 Mon–
Thu and Sun 11.30–10pm, Fri–Sat 11.30am–
11pm 🚇 U- or S-Bahn Zoologischer Garten

KNESE (€€)

plazahotel.de

This stylishly old-fashioned restaurant
serves traditional dishes such as

Königsberger Klopse (meatballs) and
calf's liver with apple sauce.

🔟 D7 ✉ Knesebeckstrasse 63 ☎ 030 88
41 34 48 🕐 Daily 11am–1am 🚇 U-Bahn
Uhlandstrasse

MARJELLCHEN (€€)

marjellchen-berlin.de

This much-loved local institution specializes in the hearty dishes of former East
Prussia, such as Pomeranian-style pork
and prunes with dumplings.

🔟 B7 ✉ Mommsenstrasse 9 ☎ 030
883 26 76 🕐 Daily from 5pm 🚇 S-Bahn
Savignyplatz

SOUPKULTUR (€)

soupkultur.de

The last word in snacks and tasty soups
makes this place justifiably popular.

🔟 D7 ✉ Kurfürstendamm 224 ☎ 030 88
62 92 82 🕐 Mon–Sat 12–6.30pm 🚇 U-Bahn
Kurfürstendamm

WINTERGARTEN IM
LITERATURHAUS (€–€€)

literaturhaus-berlin.de

This elegant city mansion dating from
1889 is the setting for both the
Literaturhaus and its fine continental-
style café-restaurant.

🔟 D7 ✉ Literaturhaus, Fasanenstrasse 23
☎ 030 882 54 14 🕐 Daily 9.30am–1am
🚇 U-Bahn Kurfürstendamm

WÜRSTCHENBUDEN

Sausage stands (_Würstchenbuden_) and
snack bars (_Schnellimbisse_) are popular
in Germany. They usually sell _Thüringer
Bratwurst_ (grilled sausage), the spicier
Krakauer and _Frankfurter Bockwurst_ and
Currywurst (fried sausage with curry ketchup). Other snacks include meatballs, served
hot or cold, called _Buletten_ in Berlin.

Potsdamer Platz

Squeezed between the southern rim of the Tiergarten and the waters of the Landwehrkanal, the district around Potsdamer Platz boasts a number of notable museums and war memorials.

Top 25

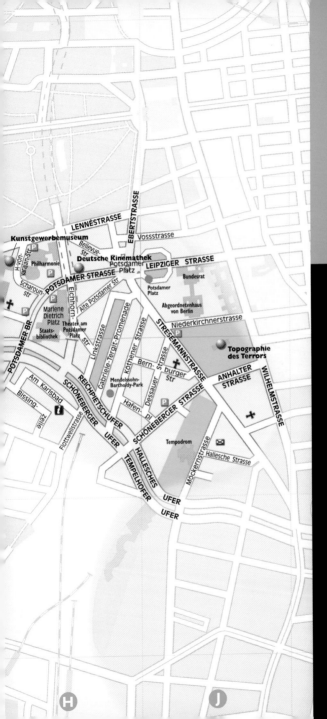

Kunstgewerbemuseum

LENNÉSTRASSE

EBERTSTRASSE

Vossstrasse

Bellevue-
Str

Deutsche Kinemathek

Philharmonie

Potsdamer
Platz

LEIPZIGER STRASSE

POTSDAMER STRASSE

H-von-
Karajan-Str

Bundesrat

Scharoun-
str

Eichhorn-
str

Alte Potsdamer Str

Potsdamer
Platz

Abgeordnetenhaus
von Berlin

Niederkirchnerstrasse

Marlene
Dietrich
Platz

Theater am
Potsdamer
Platz

STRESEMANNSTRASSE

Topographie
des Terrors

Staats-
bibliothek

Linkstrasse

Gabriele-Tergit-Promenade

Köthener Strasse

Bern-
burger
Str

Stresemann

Jerusal

POTSDAMER BR

Mendelssohn-
Bartholdy-Park

Am Karlsbad

REICHPIETSCHUFER

SCHÖNEBERGER

Bissing-
zeile

Hafen-
pl

SCHÖNEBERGER STRASSE

ANHALTER
STRASSE

WILHELMSTRASSE

UFER

Flottwellstrasse

TEMPELHOFER

Tempodrom

Möckernstrasse

Hallesche Strasse

HALLESCHES

UFER

UFER

H

J

Gemäldegalerie

HIGHLIGHTS

- *Netherlandish Proverbs,* Brueghel
- *Portrait of Enthroned Madonna and Child,* Botticelli
- *Portrait of Georg Gisze,* Holbein
- *Boy with Bird,* Rubens

TIP

- The air in the gallery is kept very dry to preserve the art, but you can take a break by the water sculpture *5–7–9 Series* by Walter de Maria in the central hall.

This gallery, in the Kulturforum complex, holds some 2,700 European paintings dating from the 13th to 18th centuries. Come here to see ground-breaking works by Rembrandt, Caravaggio and Brueghel.

Collections The Painting Gallery's collection began by bringing together various European private collections and others from royal palaces. Following World War II, the paintings were divided between East and West Berlin. In 1965, architect Rolf Gutbrod won the competition to design a complex for the museums of European art, but building work didn't start until 1985, when Gutbrod's original drawings were reworked into what is now known as the Kulturforum. The collection was eventually opened to the public in 1998.

Clockwise from far left: Rembrandt's masterpiece Moses Breaking the Tablets of the Law; *a gallery talk on the Middelburg Altar (c1450) by Rogier van der Wayden; 18th-century art in Room XII;* Malle Babbe *(c1633) by Frans Hals; there are many more Renaissance works in the basement galleries; visitors enjoying a talk*

Outstanding art Albrecht Dürer, Hans Holbein, Lucas Cranach the Elder and other German masters are well represented, as are the great Flemish artists Jan van Eyck, Rogier van der Weyden and Pieter Brueghel. Dutch baroque painting is also prominent, with several outstanding works by Rembrandt, among others. The Italian collection reads like a roll-call of great Renaissance artists: Fra Angelico, Piero della Francesca, Giovanni Bellini and Raphael. Outside, in the sculpture park, you can see works by Henry Moore and others. This large gallery is rather mazelike, which is not helped by the two room-numbering systems: Roman numerals for the larger, inner rooms and standard numbers for the smaller rooms, called cabinets, on the outside. If you do get lost, return to the central hall to get your bearings.

Topographie des Terrors

The Documentation Center (left) houses displays on the Gestapo and SS (right)

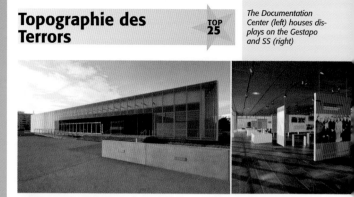

THE BASICS

topographie.de

🔲 J7

✉ Niederkirchnerstrasse 8

☎ 030 25 45 09 50

🕐 Daily 10–8 (or dusk if earlier)

🍴 Café

Ⓤ U-or S-Bahn Potsdamer Platz

🚌 129, 248, 341

♿ Free

HIGHLIGHTS

● Outdoor exhibition along trench walkway
● Remnants of original brickwork and foundations
● Section of Berlin Wall
● Documentation Center
● Models showing layout of Government Quarter 1933–45
● Bookstore

TIP

● There's a free tour in English on Sundays at 3.30—report at reception in the Documentation Center half an hour beforehand.

More than 20 years in the making, this magnificent memorial museum occupies the site that housed the headquarters of the feared Nazi security apparatus, including the SS, during the Third Reich (1939–45).

The path to dictatorship The outdoor exhibition tells the story of how the Nazis succeeded, in the space of little more than a year, in establishing a regime of terror and repression. The meticulously arranged displays of photographs and documents are set out at basement level along an excavated trench that runs parallel to a 200m (650ft) stretch of the Berlin Wall.

Silent witness Little remains of the original buildings apart form the foundations and a couple of gateposts. A lone survivor from that grim era is the former Air Ministry, a gray building across the road from the exhibition area.

Documentation Center The main exhibition is located inside the purpose-built Documentation Center. The displays here are arranged in five sections and cover the entire history of the SS (Schutzstaffel, literally Protection Squadron), the Gestapo (Geheime Staatspolizei, or Secret State Police) and the Reich Security Office from 1933 to 1945. By then, the security apparatus had spread its tentacles remorselessly across occupied Europe, operating a grisly network of concentration, extermination and labor camps, interrogation centers and "resettlement offices".

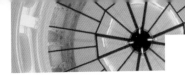

BAUHAUS-ARCHIV

bauhaus.de

The striking 1960s building that houses the Bauhaus archive of art and design is closed for renovations to celebrate the Bauhaus School's centenary in 2019, but a portion of the collection currently occupies temporary quarters in Knesebeckstrasse, off Ku'damm (Mon–Sat 10–6; free).

➕ F7 ✉ Klingelhöferstrasse 14 🕐 Closed until 2022

DEUTSCHE KINEMATHEK

deutsche-kinemathek.de

Berlin's film museum takes you on a fascinating journey through the history of German cinema, from the silent era to post-reunification revival.

➕ H6 ✉ Potsdamer Strasse 2 ☎ 030 30 09 030 🕐 Tue–Sun 10–6, Thu 10–8 🚇 U- or S-Bahn Potsdamer Platz 💷 Moderate

GEDENKSTÄTTE DEUTSCHER WIDERSTAND

gdw-berlin.de

The Memorial to German Resistance occupies the former Wehrmacht (army) headquarters, where Claus von Stauffenberg led a failed attempt to assassinate Hitler in July 1944. Stauffenberg and some of his co-plotters were executed here.

➕ G6 ✉ Stauffenbergstrasse 13–14 ☎ 030 26 99 50 00 🕐 Mon–Wed, Fri 9–6, Thu 9–8, Sat–Sun 10–6 🚇 U-Bahn Kurfürstenstrasse 🚌 M29, M48 💷 Free

KUNSTGEWERBEMUSEUM

smb.museum

The Museum of Decorative Arts covers arts, crafts, fashion and design from the Middle Ages to the present.

➕ H6 ✉ Matthäikirchplatz ☎ 030 266 42 42 42 🕐 Tue–Fri 10–6, Sat–Sun 11–6 🚇 U- or S-Bahn Potsdamer Platz 💷 Moderate

KUPFERSTICHKABINETT

smb.museum

The Engravings Room is a collection of drawings and prints by some of the great European artists.

➕ G6 ✉ Matthäikirchplatz 8 ☎ 030 266 42 42 42 🕐 Tue–Fri 10–6, Sat–Sun 11–6 🚇 U- or S-Bahn Potsdamer Platz 💷 Inexpensive

Movie buffs will love the Kinemathek, which pays homage to German film history

The Diplomatic Quarter

Tiergarten is both the old and the new diplomatic quarter of Berlin, and in recent years numerous foreign missions have settled here.

DISTANCE: 2km (1.25 miles) **ALLOW:** 1 hour

START

KLINGELHÖFERSTRASSE
✚ F6 🚌 Bus 100 Nordische Botschaften

END

POTSDAMER PLATZ
✚ J6 🚈 S-Bahn Potsdamer Platz

❶ The Nordic embassy complex at the corner of Rauchstrasse and Klingelhöferstrasse accommodates the diplomatic missions of Norway, Sweden, Denmark and Finland.

❷ Walk east along Tiergarten-strasse up to Hiroshimastrasse, which is marked by the enormous Japanese embassy on the corner, and turn right.

❸ On your left is the Italian embassy, on your right are the regional mission of Nordrhein-Westfalen and the embassy of the United Arab Emirates.

❹ Turn left at the Landwehrkanal and then left again into Hildebrandt-strasse. The big building on your right is the Ministry of Defense.

❽ Back on Tiergartenstrasse, continue east, then turn right down Bellevuestrasse to Potsdamer Platz. Stop at Weinhaus Huth, one of the few buildings here to survive the war. For years it stood alone in the no-man's land in front of the wall.

❼ Return to Tiergartenstrasse and carry on eastward to the Philharmonie (▷ 47). In front of the building turn right into Herbert-von-Karajan-Strasse. On your right is the Kulturforum, with its art gallery (▷ 42–43), decorative arts museum (▷ 45) and musical instrument museum.

❻ Turn right down Stauffenberg-strasse to visit the German Resistance memorial at No. 13–14.

❺ Head back to Tiergartenstrasse and continue east, passing the embassies of South Africa and India, the regional mission of Baden-Württemberg and the embassy of Austria.

Shopping

MALL OF BERLIN

mallofberlin.de

This spacious and airy glass-roofed mega-mall sells everything from high-end fashion to toys, and has an excellent food hall.

🚇 J6 ✉ Leipziger Platz 12 🚉 U- or S-Bahn Potsdamer Platz

MUSEUMSHOP IM KULTURFORUM

smb-webshop.de

The books, posters and souvenirs at the Museumshop are themed to reflect what's on in the on-site galleries and concert halls.

🚇 H6 ✉ Matthäikirchplatz 4 ☎ 030 266 42 42 42 🚉 U- or S-Bahn Potsdamer Platz

SONY STYLE STORE

sony.de

There are three futuristic floors where you can hear music, manipulate digital images with Sony Pictures and try out the latest Playstation.

🚇 H6 ✉ Potsdamer Strasse 4, Potsdamer Platz ☎ 030 25 75 11 88 🚉 U- or S-Bahn Potsdamer Platz

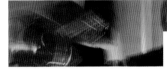

Entertainment and Nightlife

CINESTAR IMAX

cinestar.de

Berlin's biggest 3-D screen uses the latest technology and electronic glasses to bring you even closer to the action.

🚇 H6 ✉ Potsdamer Strasse 4, Potsdamer Platz ☎ 0451 703 02 00 🚉 U-Bahn or S-Bahn Potsdamer Platz

PHILHARMONIE

berliner-philharmonie.de

One of the world's top orchestras, the Berlin Philharmonic, performs in Hans Scharoun's 1960s architectural master-piece in the Kulturforum. Tickets are like gold dust so book well in advance.

🚇 H6 ✉ Herbert-von-Karajan-Strasse 1 ☎ 030 25 48 80 🚉 U- or S-Bahn Potsdamer Platz

SPIELBANK BERLIN

spielbank-berlin.de

The Spielbank Berlin, the city's only even slightly Vegas-style casino, has both gambling tables and slot machines, as well as a poker area and a show stage. The dress code is smart casual.

🚇 H6 ✉ Marlene Dietrich Platz 1, Potsdamer Platz ☎ 030 25 59 90 🕐 Daily 11am–5am 🚉 U- or S-Bahn Potsdamer Platz

VICTORIA BAR

victoriabar.de

At this chic retro bar, an impressive list of celebrity DJs and actors are attracted by the extensive classic cocktail menu and quality service.

🚇 G7 ✉ Potsdamer Strasse 102 ☎ 030 25 75 99 77 🕐 Sun–Thu 6.30pm–3am, Fri–Sat 6.30–4 🚉 U- or S-Bahn Potsdamer Platz

CINEMA

Films are usually dubbed into German. If a film is showing in its original language version it will say OV (*Originalversion*) or OmU (*Original mit Untertiteln,* original with subtitles) on the poster outside the cinema.

Where to Eat

PRICES
Prices are approximate, based on a 3-course meal for one person. €€€ over €40 €€ €20–€40 € under €20

CAFÉ EINSTEIN STAMMHAUS (€€)

cafeeinstein.com

This Viennese-style coffeehouse re-creates a prewar Berlin café atmosphere, with parquet floors and wood paneling. Enjoy a decadent continental breakfast, or come for a traditional *Wienerschnitzel* (veal escalope) with potato salad at lunchtime.

🚇 F7 ✉ Kurfürstenstrasse 58 ☎ 030 26 39 19 18 🕐 Daily 8am–midnight (meals served till 6pm) 🚇 U-Bahn Nollendorfplatz

CAFFÈ E GELATO (€)

caffe-e-gelato.de

Eat in or take out at this fantastic café and ice-cream shop on the top floor of the Potsdamer Platz Arkaden. Choose from an extensive range of ice creams and sorbets, share a towering sundae or sample the cakes and coffee.

🚇 H6 ✉ Potsdamer Platz Arkaden, Alte Potsdamer Strasse 7 ☎ 030 25 29 78 32 🕐 Mon–Thu 1–930, Fri 10–10, Sat 10am–11pm, Sun 10.30–9.30 🚇 U- or S-Bahn Potsdamer Platz

CORROBOREE (€€)

corroboree.info

Some pretty decent tucker is on offer at this shiny, ultramodern Australian restaurant and bar—you can order a kangaroo steak from the barbecue.

🚇 H6 ✉ Bellevuestrasse 5, Potsdamer Platz ☎ 030 26 10 17 05 🕐 Daily 11am–1am or later 🚇 U- or S-Bahn Potsdamer Platz

FACIL (€€€)

facil.de

Mediterranean cuisine with a French twist is served at the Hotel Mandala's Michelin-starred restaurant. You'll be treated to first-class service in this tranquil glasshouse in the bamboo-filled quadrangle at the heart of the hotel.

🚇 H6 ✉ Mandala Hotel, Potsdamer Strasse 3 ☎ 030 590 05 12 34 🕐 Mon–Fri 12–3, 7–11 🚇 U- or S-Bahn Potsdamer Platz

KAISERSAAL (€€€)

kaisersaal-berlin.de

In 1996, a beautiful ensemble of rooms known as the Kaisersaal was moved 76m (249ft) to its present location in the Sony Center. You can linger over coffee and cakes in the café or eat in the Lutter & Wegner restaurant. This gourmet establishment serves classical German-French cuisine. Reservations are essential.

🚇 H6 ✉ Bellevuestrasse 1 ☎ 030 25 75 14 54 🕐 Daily 12–midnight 🚇 U- or S-Bahn Potsdamer Platz

LINDENBRÄU (€€)

bier-genuss.berlin

Stretching over three floors above its terrace in the Sony Center, this modern brewery-restaurant serves grills and tasty *Flammkuchen* (crispy German pizzas).

🚇 H6 ✉ Bellevuestrasse 3–5 ☎ 030 25 75 12 80 🕐 Daily 11.30am–1am 🚇 U- or S-Bahn Potsdamer Platz

VOX (€€€)

vox-restaurant.de

For a culinary feast, this restaurant serves Pacific cuisines—including sushi—with a dab of Caribbean never far away.

🚇 H6 ✉ Grand Hyatt Hotel, Marlene-Dietrich-Platz ☎ 030 25 53 17 72 🕐 Daily 6.30am–midnight 🚇 U- or S-Bahn Potsdamer Platz

Kreuzberg

A multiethnic community with a large population of Turkish origin, Kreuzberg has long been seen as "alternative" Berlin. This is a great place to simply have a wander and browse the quirky independent stores, before chilling at a local café.

Top 25

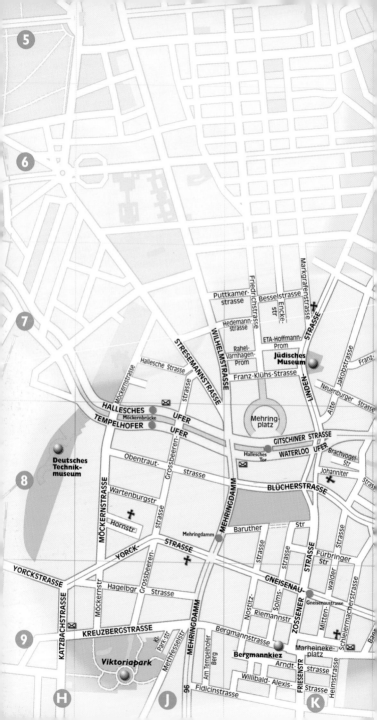

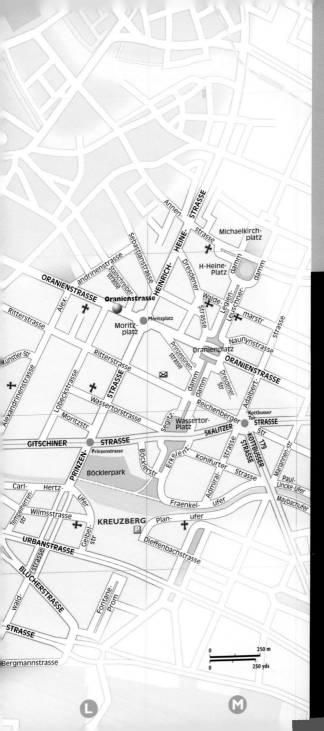

Kreuzberg

Bergmannkiez

Stroll down the busy main thoroughfare to feel the pulse of this bustling part of the city

THE BASICS

🔲 J9–L9
✉ Kreuzberg
🚇 U-Bahn
Mehringdamm,
Gneisenaustrasse,
Südstern
🚌 140
🍴 Many ethnic cafés
and restaurants

HIGHLIGHTS

● Friedrichswerdscher
cemetery
● Viktoriapark (▷ 54)
● Marheineke Markthalle
● Passionskirche
● Volkspark Hasenheide

Residents often refer to the area between Bergmannstrasse, Viktoriapark and Südstern as their *Kiez,* or neighborhood. The term has homey associations, and tourists too will feel at home roaming among its sidewalk cafés, boutiques and restaurants.

Around Marheinekeplatz The commercial heart of Bergmannstrasse is the Markthalle, a colorful covered market selling everything from fruit and vegetables to wines, cheeses, flowers and cheap clothes. Many of the eateries here have outside tables where you can soak up the Kiez's multicultural character. Before you leave, take a look at the Passionskirche, which puts on classical music concerts and poetry readings.

East–west axis While the west end of Bergmannstrasse is predominantly commercial, the area beyond the children's playground is more residential. Here shabbily genteel apartment blocks give way to a series of imposing public buildings from the same period, including the rambling Friedrichswerdersche cemetery and the old parish school opposite. Beyond is Südstern and another old survivor, the former garrison church. Two parks act like bookends at either end of Bergmannstrasse. In the west is Viktoriapark (▷ 54), actually more of a hillock with an artificial waterfall, and the evergeen Golgotha beer garden. At the eastern end of the Kiez is the Volkspark Hasenheide, popular today with picnickers and skateboarders.

Lively Oranienstrasse is lined with small independent stores and neighborhood cafés

Oranienstrasse

Known to locals simply as "O-Strasse," this 2km-long (1.5-mile) thoroughfare typifies Kreuzberg's ethnic diversity and pulsates with life. In the 1960s, O-Strasse was the epitome of radical chic, and retains its edgy feel today as residents take on the property developers.

Two worlds The main tourist sights cluster at the western end of the street, really an extension of the city center. One must-see is the Jewish Museum (▷ 54); also worth investigating is the Berlinische Galerie, an exhibition space for modern art, photography and architecture. Oranienstrasse's character changes east of Franz-Waldeck-Park and August Stüler's splendid St. Jakobi church, dating from 1845. You are now entering "Little Istanbul," the heart of Berlin's sizeable Turkish community. Soak up the atmosphere in one of the coffee houses or hookah bars; alternatively stop for lunch in Hasir's restaurant (▷ 56), founded in 1971.

Around Oranienplatz East and West Berlin used to meet at the border crossing on Heinrich-Heine-Strasse. Graffiti artists have been busy in the area. For a bit of peace and quiet, head off to Michaelkirchplatz and the Engelbecken pond, with its restful café and terrace (▷ 56). Overlooking the square is another impressive church, St. Michael, while back on Oranienstrasse, the Oranien Hof (No. 183), a residential and business complex, is a fine example of early 20th-century architecture.

THE BASICS

🚇 K6–M7 (and beyond)
✉ Kreuzberg
🚇 U-Bahn Kochstrasse, Moritzplatz, Görlitzer Bahnhof
🚌 M29, 140
🍴 Many ethnic cafés and restaurants

HIGHLIGHTS

- Berlinische Galerie
- Jüdisches Museum (▷ 54)
- Engelbecken pond
- St. Jakobi-Kirche
- Oranien Hof
- Agostino Iacurci's mural on Prinzenstrasse, near Moritzplatz

More to See

DEUTSCHES TECHNIKMUSEUM
jmberlin.de

The entertaining Technology Museum is housed in the locomotive sheds of the old Anhalter Bahnhof. There are biplanes, vintage cars, model ships, and IT; and plenty of hands-on experiences for children to try, such as playing on computers and other gadgets.

🔀 H8 ✉ Trebbiner Strasse 9 ☎ 030 90 25 40 🕐 Tue–Fri 9–5.30, Sat–Sun 10–6 🚇 U-Bahn Gleisdreieck or Möckernbrücke, S-Bahn Anhalter Bahnhof 💶 Moderate

JÜDISCHES MUSEUM
juedisches-museum-berlin.de

This controversial building, dating from 1989 and designed by Polish-born American architect Daniel Libeskind, contains an exhibition on German-Jewish history from the earliest times to the present day. A Jewish museum in Berlin has an appalling burden of history to shoulder. This fact is amplified by Libeskind's abrasive architecture (attached to an existing baroque building) and by sculptural and design elements such as the installation titled *Schalechet* (*Fallen Leaves*, 2001), by Menashe Kadishman, which depicts more than 10,000 faces hacked out of sheet steel. But there's more than the somber message of the Holocaust to take in here. The story of Germany's long and once rich Jewish heritage is told in an imaginative, interactive way.

🔀 K7 ✉ Lindenstrasse 9–14 ☎ 030 25 99 33 00 🕐 Daily 10–8 🚇 U-Bahn Kochstrasse or Hallesches Tor 🚌 M29, M41, 248 💶 Moderate

VIKTORIAPARK

Best known for Karl Friedrich Schinkel's monument to Germany's Wars of Liberation from the French (1813–15) and its artificial waterfall, this park is approached from a row of terraces and gardens. There are good views of Berlin from the Kreuzberg summit.

🔀 J9 ✉ Kreuzbergstrasse 🚇 U-Bahn Platz der Luftbrücke

Classic and modern at the Deutsches Technikmuseum

Gothic-style monument in Viktoriapark

Shopping

BAGAGE

bag-age.de

This shop sells bags of all shapes, sizes and hues—including everything from handbags and satchels to rucksacks and travel bags.

➕ K9 ✉ Bergmannstrasse 13 ☎ 030 693 89 16 🚇 U-Bahn Gneisenaustrasse

BELLA CASA

bcasa.de

Bella Casa is filled with Middle Eastern and Oriental household furnishings and fittings, interesting ornaments, pottery, different perfumes, an array of herbs and spices and more.

➕ K9 ✉ Bergmannstrasse 101 ☎ 030 694 07 84 🚇 U-Bahn Gneisenaustrasse

BELLADONNA

belladonna-naturkosmetik.de

The impressive range of natural and aromatherapy products here includes German brands such as Lavera, Logona, Dr Hauschka and Weleda. There are also oils from Primavera.

➕ K9 ✉ Bergmannstrasse 101 ☎ 030 694 37 31 🚇 U-Bahn Gneisenaustrasse

TÜRKISCHER MARKT

tuerkenmarkt.de

This intriguing market in the heart of the Turkish community offers a delicious range of choice ethnic food—including olives, cheeses and spiced chicken.

➕ M8 ✉ Maybachufer 🕐 Tue–Fri 11–6.30 🚇 U-Bahn Schönleinstrasse

Entertainment and Nightlife

GOLGATHA

golgatha-berlin.de

This popular beer garden at the south-western end of Viktoriapark turns into a disco at 10pm. It's also perfect for a morning coffee.

➕ Off map at J9 ✉ Dudenstrasse 40 ☎ 030 785 24 53 🕐 Apr–Sep daily 9am–6am; Oct–Mar dependent on weather 🚇 U-Bahn Platz der Luftbrücke

LIMONADIER

limonadier.de

Popular for its laid-back 1920s ambience and friendly bar staff, Limonadier serves up inventive cocktails and, of course, homemade lemonade.

➕ K9 ✉ Nostitzstrasse 12 ☎ 0170 601 20 20 🕐 Mon–Thu 7pm–2am, Fri–Sat 7pm–3am 🚇 U-Bahn Mehringdamm

YORCKSCHLÖSSCHEN

yorckschloesschen.de

This evergeen venue for live jazz and blues also serves meals and local beers, both inside and on the (usually crowded) trerrace. Check the website for performance times.

➕ H9 ✉ Yorckstrasse 15 ☎ 030 215 80 70 🕐 Mon–Sat 5pm–3am, Sun 11–3pm, 5pm–3am 🚇 U-Bahn Mehringdamm

LOCAL TIPPLES

A local drink is *Berliner Weisse*, beer with a dash of raspberry or woodruff syrup *(mit Grün)*. *Herva mit Mosel* is a peculiar blend of white wine with maté tea; Berliners consume millions of glasses of the drink annually. Hardened drinkers prefer *Korn*—frothy beer with a schnapps chaser.

Where to Eat

PRICES

Prices are approximate, based on a 3-course meal for one person.
€€€ over €40
€€ €20–€40
€ under €20

AMRIT (€€)

amrit.de

The warm surroundings, attentive staff and excellent food have long made this Indian restaurant a popular choice for both locals and visitors.

⊞ Off map, east of M7 ⊠ Oranienstrasse 202 ☎ 030 612 55 50 ⊕ Daily 12pm–1am ⊜ U-Bahn Görlitzer Bahnhof

BERGMANN CURRY (€)

bergmann-curry.de

This is the place to try Berlin's unusual contribution to the world of fast food: the *Currywurst*—basically a sausage smothered in ketchup and sprinkled with curry powder. The difference here is that all the ingredients are organic.

⊞ K9 ⊠ Bergmannstrasse 88 ☎ 030 50 56 51 54 ⊕ Daily 12–8 ⊜ U-Bahn Gneisenaustrasse

CAFÉ AM ENGELBECKEN (€)

cafe-am-englebecken.de

As you breakfast on the sunny terrace overlooking the pond, it is hard to believe that this site was once part of the Berlin Wall death strip.

⊞ M7 ⊠ Michaelkirchplatz ☎ 030 64 31 51 34 ⊕ Daily 10am–midnight ⊜ U-Bahn Heinrich-Heine-Strasse

DOLDEN MÄDEL (€€)

doldenmaedel-berlin.de

A large, busy restaurant with a summer garden, this newcomer to the scene serves homemade burgers, schnitzels, sausages and vegan and vegetarian choices, washed down with craft beers.

⊞ J9 ⊠ Mehringdamm 80 ☎ 030 77 32 62 13 ⊕ Sun–Thu 11.30am–12.30am, Fri–Sat 11.30am–1.30am ⊜ U-Bahn Mehringdamm

HASIR (€–€€)

hasir.de

This welcoming Turkish restaurant claims to have created the world's first döner kebab, in 1971.

⊞ M7 ⊠ Adalbertstrasse 10 ☎ 030 614 23 73 ⊕ Daily 24 hours ⊜ U-Bahn Kottbusser Tor

HENNE (€€)

henne-berlin.de

A long-time Kreuzberg institution, this old-fashioned pub-style establishment specializes in tender roast organic chicken washed down with a local beer.

⊞ M7 ⊠ Leuschnerdamm 25 ☎ 030 614 77 30 ⊕ Tue–Sun 5–11 ⊜ U-Bahn Moritzplatz

TAVERNA ATHENE (€€)

taverna-athene-de

This large, family-run business dishes up meze platters, grilled meat and fish dishes, beers, wines and retsina. A TV rooms shows major soccer games.

⊞ J8 ⊠ Tempelhofer Ufer 12 ☎ 030 251 60 69 ⊕ Tue–Sun 3pm–midnight ⊜ U-Bahn Möckernbrücke

LITTLE ISTANBUL

Kreuzberg, near the middle of Berlin, has the largest Turkish community outside Istanbul. In the bustling areas of Kottbusser Tor and Schlesisches Tor, dozens of restaurants offer inexpensive and interesting Anatolian cuisine. There's also a growing range of national cuisines to be found here, especially from Asia and North Africa.

Unter den Linden

Encompassing the boulevard Unter den Linden at one end and the leafy Tiergarten at the other, this district is a study in contrasts and has a wealth of historic, cultural and architectural assets.

Top 25

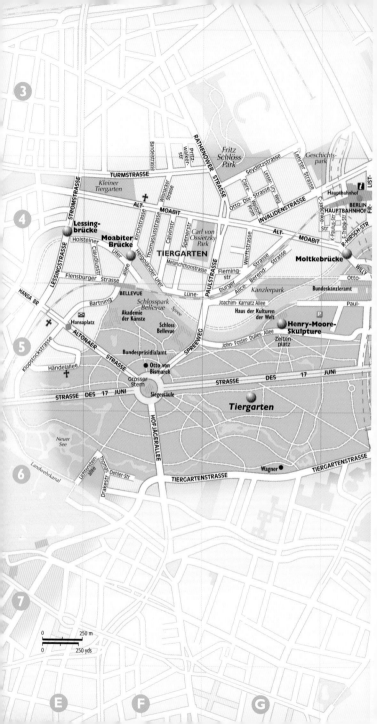

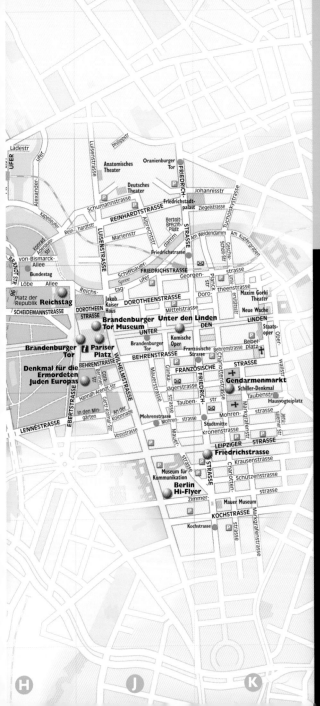

Unter den Linden

Brandenburger Tor

Gottfried Schadow's bronze sculpture tops this iconic gate

THE BASICS

✚ J5
✉ Pariser Platz
🚇 U- and S-Bahn Brandenburger Tor
🚌 100, TXL
♿ None
🎫 Free

Brandenburger Tor Museum
✉ Pariser Platz 4a
☎ 030 23 60 78 436
🕐 Sat–Sun 10–8
🎫 Moderate

HIGHLIGHTS

● The Quadriga
● Classical reliefs
● Adjoining classical pavilions
● View down Unter den Linden
● View down Strasse des 17. Juni
● "Room of Silence" (in pavilion)
● Pariser Platz (▷ 64)
● Brandenburger Tor Museum

The Brandenburg Gate began life as a humble tollgate, marking the city's western boundary. Today it symbolizes the reconciliation of East and West and is the perfect backdrop for commemorative events, celebrations and rock concerts.

Gate of peace? The gate is the work of Karl Gotthard Langhans and dates from 1788–91. Its neoclassical style echoes the ancient entrance to the Acropolis in Athens, on which it is fashioned. Conceived as an Arch of Peace, the Brandenburg Gate has more frequently been used to glorify martial values, as in 1933, when the Nazis' torchlight procession through the arch was intended to mark the beginning of the 1,000-year Reich.

Viktoria The Quadriga, a sculpture depicting the goddess Viktoria driving her chariot, was added to the gate by Johann Gottfried Schadow in 1794. In 1806, following the Prussian defeat at Jena, it was moved to Paris by Napoleon. When it was brought back in triumph less than a decade later, Karl Friedrich Schinkel added a wreath of oak leaves and the original Iron Cross to Viktoria's standard.

Brandenburger Tor Museum This new attraction offers visitors a potted history of Berlin from the vantage point of its most famous "silent witness." Go time traveling in the immersive cinema, then catch your breath in the adjoining photo exhibition.

Named for King Friedrich I of Prussia and laid out in the 18th century, Friedrichstrasse bisects the central city on a north–south axis. It was itself cut in two by the East–West cleft of the Berlin Wall during the days of Berlin's division.

Street of dreams Stretching from the Oranienburger Tor to the Hallesches Tor, this is a long street, crossing the River Spree and Unter den Linden (▷ 68) on the way. Shoppers flock to Friedrichstrasse for retail therapy, or to enjoy the area's top restaurants. The flagship French chain store Galeries Lafayette (▷ 70) is just one of the stellar names. Some of the smaller streets that traverse Friedrichstrasse, such as Französische Strasse, have respectable shopping, dining and entertainment scenes of their own. Roughly midway down, just off its eastern face, is Gendarmenmarkt (▷ 62–63), Berlin's most handsome square and site of the impressive Konzerthaus (▷ 71).

Cold War games Friedrichstrasse was once one of the flashpoints of the East–West confrontation. The famous American Checkpoint Charlie was at the lower end of Friedrichstrasse, at Zimmerstrasse. US and Red Army tanks once squared off across the brief space of that street, where tourists now snap each other's picture. The fascinating Haus am Checkpoint Charlie museum explores some of the ingenious methods people found to escape from East Germany, both in Berlin and across the Baltic.

THE BASICS

➕ K7–J4
✉ Friedrichstrasse
🚇 U- and S-Bahn Friedrichstrasse; U-Bahn Französische Strasse, Stadtmitte or Kochstrasse
🚌 M1, M12, M29, M41, 100, 147, 200
🍴 Many restaurants and cafés

HIGHLIGHTS

● Galeries Lafayette (▷ 70)
● Französische Strasse
● Checkpoint Charlie (▷ 18)
● Unter den Linden (▷ 68)
● Gendarmenmarkt (▷ 62–63)

Gendarmenmarkt

TOP 25

HIGHLIGHTS

- Konzerthaus
- Statue of Schiller
- Apollo in his chariot
- Deutscher Dom
- Französischer Dom
- **Französischer Dom**
- Balustrade view
- Carillon

TIP

● Gendarmenmarkt is every bit as attractive after dark, with its illuminated grand neoclassical buildings. If you want to shoot some serious pictures at this time, you'll need a tripod.

This beautiful square comes as a pleasant surprise for visitors who associate Berlin with imperial bombast and Prussian marching bands. Climb the tower of the Französischer Dom for superb views of the Friedrichstadt district.

Konzerthaus Known originally as the Schauspielhaus (theater), the Konzerthaus was designed by Karl Friedrich Schinkel in 1821. Its predecessor was destroyed by fire during a rehearsal of Schiller's play *The Robbers*, so it is fitting that the playwright's monument stands outside. When the building was restored in the early 1980s after being severely damaged in World War II, the original stage and auditorium made way for a concert hall with a capacity of 1,850—hence the change of name. The facade,

From left: the elegant classical architecture of the Gendarmenmakt; the colonnaded Konzerthaus with the fine dome of the Französischer Dom (French Cathedral) beyond

however, retains Schinkel's original design. Look for the sculpture of Apollo in his chariot.

Two cathedrals The twin French and German churches (Französischer Dom and Deutscher Dom) occupy opposite ends of the square. The architect Karl von Gontard was described as an ass by Frederick the Great; one of the complementary cupolas collapsed in 1781. A small museum in the Deutscher Dom charts the history of German democracy from the 19th century to the present with photographs, film and a variety of objects. A museum in the Französischer Dom tells the story of the hard-working Huguenots who settled in Berlin in the 17th century after fleeing persecution in France. The church (minus its baroque tower, a later addition) was built for them.

THE BASICS

franzoesischer-dom.de

➕ K5–K6

☎ Französischer Dom: 030 229 17 60. Deutscher Dom: 030 22 73 04 31

🕐 Französischer Dom: daily 10–7. Huguenot Museum: closed for restoration until late 2019. Deutscher Dom: Tue–Sun 10–6 (7 May–Sep)

🚇 U-Bahn Stadtmitte, Französische Strasse

🚌 M48, 147, 347

💶 Inexpensive

Pariser Platz

TOP 25

The square's organ grinders and ornate lampposts are reminders of a bygone age

UNTER DEN LINDEN TOP 25

THE BASICS

⊞ J5
✉ Pariser Platz
🍽 Cafés and restaurants on Unter den Linden
🚇 U- or S-Bahn Brandenburger Tor
🚌 100, 200, TXL
🎟 Free

HIGHLIGHTS

● Brandenburger Tor (▷ 60)
● Unter den Linden (▷ 68)
● Akademie der Künste
● Brandenburger Tor Museum (▷ 60)
● Information boards providing history and images of the square as it was in the past

The square was named after the French capital in 1814, when the Allies, including Prussia, occupied Paris after seeing off Napoleon (or so they thought).

Risen from the ashes Photographs in the Brandenburg Gate Museum (▷ 60) show what the elegant square looked like in its imperial heyday, but it bit the dust during World War II. With the Berlin Wall then being constructed right next to it, the square was unable to recover any of its former glory. It remained a wasteland until the reunified Berlin's booming 1990s, when the square was transformed.

New look Notable modern buildings are the Adlon Hotel, the DG Bank, the French, British and US embassies, the Akademie der Künste (Academy of the Arts) and the Dresdner Bank. The oldest embassy in the vicinity belongs to Russia. Originally the Soviet Embassy, it dates from 1950 and was designed in the Stalinist wedding cake style then popular. The two rectangular gardens (with fountains) at the northern and southern quadrants replicate the original plan for the square.

Passing pedestrians The square was once a vibrant, lively place but now has a quieter atmosphere. There is, however, a constant stream of people moving between the Brandenburger Tor (▷ 60), which forms the square's western outlet, and the watering holes and cultural venues along Unter den Linden.

Reichstag

Size and space are awesome both inside and outside of this striking building

Take the walkway to the top of Sir Norman Foster's impressive glass dome to get an inside look at the seat of the German parliament.

Parliament building The original Reichstag was built between 1884 and 1894 by Paul Wallot as the seat of the imperial parliament. The building was completely devastated as a result of heavy fighting during World War II. After extensive restoration, the building was handed to the federal administration in 1973, and the first session of the reunified Bundestag (federal parliament) was held here in 1990.

The dome In June 1993, the British architect Sir Norman Foster was awarded the commission to restore the Reichstag. Foster preserved the original features and functions of the building, while adding glass walls, and a glass roof and chamber that bring light into the heart of the structure. Foster's dome is visible for miles around and has a powerful presence on Berlin's skyline. It has also become a symbol of popular rule, and every day thousands of people climb to the top. Visitors are reflected in the central mirrored funnel as they walk up the gently sloping spiral walkway. From the top, you can look down into the chamber, a view representing open democratic rule. Information panels around the base of the funnel document the history of the Reichstag, and you can walk out of the dome onto the roof terrace to appreciate the view over the city.

THE BASICS

bundestag.de

✚ H5

✉ Platz der Republik 1

☎ 030 22 70

🕐 Apr–Oct daily 8–8; Nov–Mar daily 8–6

Ⓤ U-Bahn Bundestag

🚌 M41, 100, TXL

♿ Free

HIGHLIGHTS

● Views of the city from Sir Norman Foster's glass dome
● View a sitting of the Bundestag from the gallery
● *Black, Red and Gold* (1999) artwork of German flag in the west hall

TIP

● When booking a visit, you must bring your passport or other valid ID with you. When you arrive at the ticket office, you will be asked to choose a time slot—be prepared to be flexible, as places are limited.

Tiergarten

HIGHLIGHTS

- Zoologischer Garten (Zoo Berlin, ▷ 34)
- Kongresshalle
- Carillon
- Bismarck monument
- Schloss Bellevue
- Neuer See
- Englischer Garten

TIP

- Reaching the top of the Siegessäule is a challenge, but the view of the Tiergarten district from up there should make the climb worthwhile

Boating, strolling, jogging, summer concerts—this huge park in the heart of Berlin offers all this and more, while the diplomatic quarter south of Tiergartenstrasse is worth exploring for its amazing architecture.

Hunting ground *Tiergarten* means "animal garden," recalling a time when the park was stocked with wild boar and deer for the Prussian aristocracy. It was landscaped by Peter Joseph Lenné in the 1830s and still bears his imprint—even though the park was almost totally destroyed in World War II.

Siegessäule The Siegessäule (Victory Column) occupies a prime site on Strasse des 17. Juni, although it originally stood in front of the

Clockwise from far left: the Siegessäule victory column; Berlin's green lung, the Tiergarten, provides an essential space for city dwellers to relax; the Siegessäule still bears scars from gunfire during World War II; view from the top of the Siegessäule toward the Brandenburg Gate; many waterways wend their way through the park

Reichstag. Erected in 1873 to commemorate Prussian victories against Denmark, Austria and France, the 67m (220ft) column is decorated with captured cannon. "Gold Else," the victory goddess on the summit, beloved of Berliners, waves her laurel wreath wryly towards Paris.

War heroes and revolutionaries The heroes of the Wars of Unification—Count Otto von Bismarck and Generals Helmuth von Moltke and Albrecht von Roon—are feted with statues to the north of the Siegessäule. Memorials to two Communist revolutionaries, Karl Liebknecht and Rosa Luxemburg, stand beside the Landwehrkanal near Lichtenstein-allee. Luxemburg's body was dumped in the canal in 1919 by members of the right-wing Freikorps; she'd been shot after an abortive uprising.

THE BASICS

Siegessäule

✚ F5

✉ Grosser Stern, Strasse des 17. Juni

☎ 030 391 29 61

🕐 Apr–Oct Mon–Fri 9.30–6.30, Sat–Sun 9.30–7; Nov–Mar Mon–Fri 10–5, Sat–Sun 10–5.30

🚉 S-Bahn Bellevue

🚌 100, 106, 187

♿ None

💷 Inexpensive

❓ Viewing platform (no elevator)

Unter den Linden

TOP 25

The classically styled opera house (right) presides over eastern Unter den Linden (left)

THE BASICS

🖽 J5–K5
✉ Unter den Linden 2
☎ Deutsches Historisches Museum: 030 20 30 40. Hedwigskirche: dhm.de
🕓 Deutsches Historisches Museum: daily 10–6.
Ⓤ U- or S-Bahn Brandenburger Tor, U-Bahn Französische Strasse
🚌 100, 200
♿ Deutsches Historisches Museum: moderate

HIGHLIGHTS

● Staatsoper Unter den Linden (▷ 71)
● Facade of Alte-Königliche Bibliothek
● Statue of Frederick the Great
● Humboldt University
● Neue Wache
● Zeughaus (see warriors' masks in the Schlüterhof)

The avenue "Under the Linden Trees," once the heart of imperial Berlin and still the city's most famous street, is lined with neoclassical and baroque buildings.

Forum Fridericianum Frederick the Great presides over the eastern end of Unter den Linden. His equestrian statue, by Daniel Christian Rauch, stands next to Bebelplatz, once known as the Forum Fridericianum and intended to evoke the grandeur of imperial Rome. Dominating the square is Georg von Knobelsdorff's opera house, the Staatsoper (▷ 71). Facing it is the Alte Bibliothek (Old Library), completed in 1780. Here, in 1933, Nazi propaganda chief Josef Goebbels publicly burned the works of ideological opponents. Just south of Bebelplatz is the Roman Catholic cathedral, the Hedwigskirche, whose classical lines echo the Pantheon in Rome.

Zeughaus Frederick's civic project was never completed, but the buildings on the opposite side of Unter den Linden keep up imperial appearances. The Humboldt University was designed by Johann Boumann as a palace for Frederick the Great's brother in 1748. Next comes the Neue Wache (New Guardhouse), designed by Schinkel in 1818 to complement Johann Nering's 1695 baroque palace, the Zeughaus (Arsenal), home of the Deutsches Historisches Museum (German History Museum). The superb dying warriors sculptures in the courtyard are by Andreas Schlüter.

More to See

BERLIN HI-FLYER

air-service-berlin.de

A huge, secured helium balloon rises up to a height of 150m (492ft) and crosses the city center for bird's-eye views.

➕ J6 ✉ Corner of Wilhelmstrasse and Zimmerstrasse ☎ 030 53 21 53 21 🕐 Apr–Oct daily 10–10; Nov–Mar 11–6 Ⓜ U-Bahn Mohrenstrasse or Kochstrasse 💶 Expensive

BRIDGES OVER THE SPREE

At the Spreebogen (Spree Bend), you can walk along the embankment to take in three historic bridges. The Moltkebrücke is named for a hero of the Franco-Prussian War of 1870. Note the sculptures of cherubic pseudo-Roman soldiers decorating the parapet. Soviet troops crossed this bridge in 1945 before storming the Reichstag. The Moabiter Brücke of 1864 is famous for its guardian bears. Scenes from playwright Gotthold Lessing's (1729–81) dramas decorate the piers of Lessingbrücke, connecting Moabit district with the Hansaviertel.

Moltkebrücke ➕ H4 ✉ Willy-Brandt-Strasse Ⓢ S-Bahn Hauptbahnhof; Moabiter Brücke ➕ F4 ✉ Bellevue Ufer Ⓢ S-Bahn Bellevue; Lessingbrücke ➕ E4 ✉ Lessingstrasse Ⓜ U-Bahn Hansaplatz, S-Bahn Bellevue

DENKMAL FÜR DIE ERMORDETEN JUDEN EUROPAS

stiftung-denkmal.de

Architect Peter Eisenman's memorial to the murdered Jews of Europe is an impressive maze of more than 2,700 stelae. It is a place of (not always quiet) reflection.

➕ J5 ✉ Between Ebertstrasse and Cora-Berliner-Strasse ☎ 030 26 39 430 🕐 Memorial: permanently; information center: Apr–Sep Tue–Sun 10–8; Oct–Mar Tue–Sun 10–7 Ⓢ U- or S-Bahn Brandenburger Tor 🚌 M41, 123, 200, TXL 💶 Free

HENRY-MOORE-SKULPTURE

Henry Moore's statue *Large Butterfly* (1984) "flutters" gently over a lake outside the Kongresshalle in the Tiergarten.

➕ G5 ✉ John-Foster-Dulles-Allee 🚌 100

Stelae field at the Denkmal für die Ermordeten Juden Europas

Looking down the River Spree, from Bellevue to the Moabiter Brücke

Shopping

ANTIK- UND BUCHMARKT AM BODEMUSEUM

antik-buchmarkt.de

Browse through books, records, CDs and bric-a-brac on the stalls on the Spree embankment.

K4 ✉ Am Kupfergraben ☎ 0171 710 16 62 🕐 Sat–Sun 11–5 🚇 U- or S-Bahn Friedrichstrasse

BERLE'S TRENDS AND GIFTS

berles-berlin.de

If you're not a fan of traditional souvenirs, try the novelty gifts here, from cuckoo clocks to cereal dispensers.

K6 ✉ Mohrenstrasse 50 ☎ 030 20 67 39 30 🚇 U-Bahn Stadtmitte

BERLINER KUNSTMARKT

The Berlin art market specializes in art, crafts and nostalgia—for the most part paintings, drawings and antiques.

K5 ✉ Am Zeughaus 1–2 ☎ 0172 301 88 73 🕐 Sat–Sun 11–5 🚇 U- or S-Bahn Friedrichstrasse

BÜRGELHAUS

echt-buergel.de

Here you will find the distinctive blue and cream pottery that is produced in the German region of Thüringia. The prices are very reasonable.

J5 ✉ Friedrichstrasse 154 ☎ 030 20 45 26 95 🚇 U- or S-Bahn Friedrichstrasse

DUSSMANN: DAS KULTURKAUFHAUS

kulturkaufhaus.de

This huge book and record store is ideal for last-minute present buying. Where CDs are concerned, if they don't have it here, you won't find it anywhere. Stays open until 10pm.

K5 ✉ Friedrichstrasse 90 ☎ 030 20 25 11 11 🚇 U- or S-Bahn Friedrichstrasse

GALERIES LAFAYETTE

galerieslafayette.de

This is the first and only branch of the iconic Parisian department store in Germany. Behind the smooth glass facade are five floors of French flair and a mouthwatering food hall.

K5 ✉ Friedrichstrasse 76–78 ☎ 030 20 94 80 🕐 Daily 10–8 🚇 U-Bahn Französische Strasse

HAUS AM CHECKPOINT CHARLIE

mauermuseum.de

This is the only place in Berlin where you can still find an authentic piece of the Wall to buy, as well as military insignia and much more.

K6 ✉ Friedrichstrasse 43–45 ☎ 030 253 72 50 🚇 U-Bahn Kochstrasse

MEISSEN BOUTIQUE

meissen.com/de

Lovers of fine china will enjoy browsing the handmade figurines and tableware from the famous Meissen factory.

J5 ✉ Unter den Linden 39 ☎ 030 22 67 90 28 🚇 U-Bahn Französische Strasse

RAUSCH SCHOKOLADENHAUS

A luxury chocolate shop and confectioner founded in the 19th century, which sells all manner of delicious goodies for chocaholics.

K6 ✉ Charlottenstrasse 60 ☎ 030 20 45 84 43 🚇 U-Bahn Stadtmitte

RITTER SPORT BUNTE SCHOKOWELT

ritter-sport.de

The racks of brightly packaged chocolate bars here are a treat for the eye, and you can also create your own flavor (allow 40 minutes setting time).

K5 ✉ Französische Strasse 24 ☎ 030 20 09 50 810 🚇 U-Bahn Französische Strasse

Entertainment and Nightlife

ADMIRALSPALAST
mehr.de

During the 1920s, this was the most famous theater in Berlin. Now beautifully restored, it is again a wonderful stage for rock concerts and musicals.

➕ J4 ✉ Friedrichstrasse 101 ☎ 030 22 50 70 00 🚇 U-or S-Bahn Friedrichstrasse

BERLINER ENSEMBLE
berliner-ensemble.de

Playwright Bertolt Brecht (author of *The Threepenny Opera*) founded this famous theater company with his wife Helene Weigel in 1949.

➕ J4 ✉ Bertolt-Brecht-Platz 1 ☎ 030 28 40 80 🚇 U-or S-Bahn Friedrichstrasse

FRIEDRICHSTADT-PALAST
palast.berlin.de

This most famous nightspot in Berlin has a long tradition. On the main stage, entertainment includes variety acts and a floor show from its own modern dance company; the small revue stage is more intimate.

➕ J4 ✉ Friedrichstrasse 107 ☎ 030 23 26 23 27 🚇 U-Bahn Oranienburger Tor

HAUS DER KULTUREN DER WELT
hkw.de

The House of World Cultures in the Tiergarten hosts exhibitions and media events as well as concerts showcasing world music.

➕ G5 ✉ John-Foster-Dulles-Allee 10 ☎ 030 39 78 70 🚇 U-or S-Bahn Brandenburger Tor

KOMISCHE OPER BERLIN
komische-oper-berlin.de

Catch modern, inventive productions of opera, dance and musical theater at the Berlin Comic Opera.

➕ J5 ✉ Behrenstrasse 55–57 ☎ 030 20 26 00 🚇 U-Bahn Französische Strasse

KONZERTHAUS
konzerthaus.de

The home of the Konzerthausorchester Berlin is in the magnificent neoclassical theater designed by architect Karl Friedrich Schinkel in 1818. The music ranges from symphonies to chamber music, lunchtime concerts and early evening jazz.

➕ K5 ✉ Gendarmenmarkt 2 ☎ 030 203 09 23 33 🚇 U-Bahn Französische Strasse

NEWTON BAR
newton-bar.de

Designer good looks extend from the racy Helmut Newton posters to the black leather armchairs—and to the cocktail-sipping clientele. Cigar fanciers can enjoy a Cuban smoke in the separate cigar lounge.

➕ K6 ✉ Charlottenstrasse 57 ☎ 030 20 29 54 21 🚇 U-Bahn Französische Strasse

STAATSOPER UNTER DEN LINDEN
staatsoper-berlin.de

The best of both homegrown and international opera and ballet are performed in a beautiful baroque concert hall. Built in the reign of Frederick the Great, it reopened in 2017 after an extensive program of renovation. Tours of the building are available, but must be booked in advance.

➕ K5 ✉ Unter den Linden 7 ☎ 030 20 35 40 🚇 U-Bahn Hausvogteiplatz

---

FRIEDRICHSTRASSE

Before World War II, this was Berlin's entertainment district, filled with music halls and theaters. Friedrichstrasse suffered badly in World War II and the subsequent partition, but since reunification has been almost totally rebuilt to become a vibrant shopping and cultural hub.

Where to Eat

BOCCA DI BACCO (€€€)

boccadibacco.de

This is the place to go for gourmet
Italian food. The menu is classic, the
address exclusive and the staff are
friendly and welcoming.

➕ K5 ✉ Friedrichstrasse 167–168 ☎ 030 20
67 28 28 🕐 Mon–Sat 12–12, Sun 6pm–midnight 🚇 U-Bahn Französische Strasse

BORCHARDT (€€€)

borchardt-restaurant.de

With historical roots going back to 1853,
this fine European restaurant is one of
the most venerable dining establishments in town.

➕ K5 ✉ Französische Strasse 47 ☎ 030
81 88 62 62 🕐 Daily 12–12 🚇 U-Bahn
Französische Strasse

CAFÉ EINSTEIN (€€)

cafeeinstein.com

Berlin's café tradition has been revived
with fine coffees and teas, homemade
Apfelstrudel, and a large and creative
breakfast menu, all served in an art nou-
veau-style interior or outside in summer.

➕ J5 ✉ Unter den Linden 42 ☎ 030 204
36 32 🕐 Daily 7am–10pm 🚇 U- or S-Bahn
Brandenburger Tor

COOKIES CREAM (€€€)

cookiescream.com

Chef Stephan Hentschel creates healthy
vegetarian alternatives to the meat-
based cuisine of Germany in his stylish
restaurant behind Unter den Linden.

➕ J5 ✉ Behrenstrasse 55 ☎ 030 27 49
29 40 🕐 Tue–Sat from 6pm 🚇 U-Bahn
Französische Strasse

LEPOPULAIRE (€€)

db-palaispopulaire.com

The café in the PalaisPopulaire event
and exhibition space serves delicious
homemade cakes and pastries, and also
offers a brunch and lunch menu.

➕ K5 ✉ Unter den Linden 5 ☎ 030 20 20
930 🕐 Wed–Mon 9am–11pm 🚇 U-Bahn
Französische Strasse

LUTTER & WEGNER (€€€)

l-w-berlin.de

This historic 19th-century restaurant
serves Austrian and German cuisine;
there is a wine bar and outdoor seating
on the historic Gendarmenmarkt.

➕ K6 ✉ Charlottenstrasse 56 ☎ 030 202
95 40 🕐 Daily 11am–midnight 🚇 U-Bahn
Französische Strasse

NANTE-ECK (€€)

nante-eck.de

The Altberliner chain has re-created the
ambience of a traditional restaurant
from the 1920s, but the menu offers a
choice of modern dishes or hearty
Berlin favorites such as *Eisbeinsülze*
(jellied pork).

➕ J5 ✉ Unter den Linden 35 ☎ 030 22
48 72 57 🕐 Daily 9am–midnight 🚇 U-Bahn
Französische Strasse

GERMAN WINES

Germany is divided into 13 distinct wine-
growing regions, mainly along the Rhine and
Moselle river valleys. Nearly all the wine is
white, relying heavily on the Müller-Thurgau
and Riesling grapes. Red wines are not generally held in high esteem and not usually
consumed locally.

Alexanderplatz

The UNESCO World Heritage Site of Museumsinsel is not far from Alexanderplatz. But the core of the former East Berlin, beside the River Spree, has far more to offer than just museum-hopping.

3

4

5

6

7

Linien- strasse

Grosse August

Grosse Hamburger

Museum The Kennedys

ORANIEN- **BURGER**

Neue Synagoge

Krausnickstr

Oranienburger Strasse

STRASSE

Tuch- olsky-

ziegelstr

Kl

Monbijoustrasse

Monbijoupark

Bode- museum

Pergamon- museum

Am Kupfergraben

Alte National- galerie

Bodestrasse

Museumsinsel

Altes Museum

Deutsches Historisches Museum

Am Zeughaus

Neue Wache

Schlossbrücke

P

LEIPZIGER

Krausenstrasse

Schützenstrasse

Zimmerstrasse

Axel-

Junkerstr

Fellner-

0   250 m

0   250 yds

H

J

K

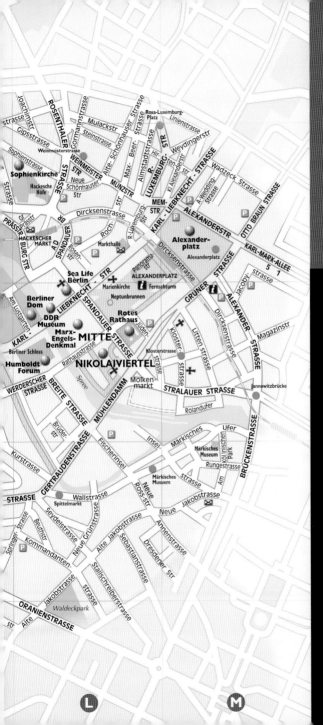

Alexanderplatz

The TV tower (left); the World Time Clock (middle) and trams (right) feature in the square

TOP 25

ALEXANDERPLATZ TOP 25

THE BASICS

tv-turm.de

➕ M4

☎ Marienkirche: 030 24 75 95 10

🕐 Fernsehturm: Mar–Oct daily 9am–midnight; Nov–Feb 10am–midnight. Marienkirche: Apr–Dec daily 10–6; Jan–Mar daily 10–4

🍴 Cafés

Ⓤ U- or S-Bahn Alexanderplatz

🚌 M48, 100, 200, TXL

♿ Fernsehturm: expensive. Marienkirche: moderate

HIGHLIGHTS

● Fernsehturm
● Rotes Rathaus (City Hall)
● World Time Clock
● Neptune Fountain
● Forum Hotel
● Kaufhof department store
● Marienkirche
● *Totentanz (Dance of Death)* wall painting

"Alex," as Berliners affectionately call this historic old marketplace, has won back a good deal of its charm with new and revamped buildings after its years as a showpiece of socialist architecture.

Historic square Alexanderplatz is named after Tsar Alexander I, who once reviewed troops here. The square was colonized by Berlin's burgeoning working class in the middle of the 19th century. Crime flourished, so it is no accident that the police headquarters was nearby.

TV tower The Fernsehturm rises like an unlovely flower from the middle of the square. Its virtue is its great height, which at 362m (1,188ft) exceeds even that of Paris's Eiffel Tower. Take the turbolift up on a fine day for panoramic city views from the viewing platform and the rotating Telecafé restaurant.

Other attractions In the square's southwestern quadrant, the spectacular Neptunbrunnen (Neptune Fountain), which was a gift to Kaiser Wilhelm II in 1891, originally stood in Schlossplatz. Its focal point is a massive bronze sculpture of the Roman god of the sea. Around the rim sit female statues representing the rivers Rhine, Oder, Elbe and Weichsel (Vistula). The Marienkirche has a 15th-century nave and a lantern tower added by Karl Gotthard Langhans in 1790. An epidemic of the plague in 1484 is commemorated in a large medieval wall painting, *Totentanz (Dance of Death)*.

The ornate decoration (left), and the imposing exterior, of the Berliner Dom (right)

Berliner Dom

For evidence of imperial pretension, look no further than Berlin's Protestant cathedral. The vast vault contains the sarcophagi of more than 90 members of the Hohenzollern dynasty.

Cathedral Architect Julius Raschdorff built the Berliner Dom over the site of a smaller imperial chapel. The existing cathedral was completed in 1905 and opened in the presence of Kaiser Wilhelm II. Inside, the most impressive feature is the High Renaissance dome, which is 74m (243ft) high, supported by pillars of Silesian sandstone and decorated with mosaics by Anton von Werner. The dome is reached by climbing 270 steps. The cathedral was badly damaged during World War II, but restoration started in 1974 and it is now well advanced; work on the stained-glass windows has been completed.

Destroyed by Allied bombs The name of the square, Lustgarten, derives from the former pleasure garden that stood just outside the cathedral on Museumsinsel. The site, where Prussia's first potatoes were planted in 1649, is now covered by grass and paving. Opposite stood the enormous Berliner Stadtschloss, dating from the early 18th century and designed by Andreas Schlüter and Johann Eosander von Goethe; it was destroyed in World War II. Today, the Humboldt Forum (▷ 82), an ambitious new project now nearing completion, occupies the Stadtschloss site.

THE BASICS

berlinerdom.de
✚ L5
✉ Am Lustgarten
☎ 030 20 26 91 36
🕐 Mon–Sat 9–7, Sun 12–7; also for concerts
🍴 None
🚇 U- and S-Bahn Alexanderplatz, S-Bahn Hackescher Markt
🚌 M48, 100, 200
♿ Moderate

HIGHLIGHTS

● High Renaissance–style facade
● Baptism chapel
● Imperial staircase
● Sarcophagi
● Dome 74m (234ft) high
● Figures above altar
● Viewing gallery
● Humboldt Forum
● Lustgarten

ALEXANDERPLATZ TOP 25

Museumsinsel

HIGHLIGHTS

● View of Altes Museum from the Lustgarten
● Rotunda of Altes Museum
● *Unter den Linden*, Franz Krüger (Alte Nationalgalerie)
● *Portrait of Frederick the Great at Potsdam*, Adolph Menzel (Alte Nationalgalerie)
● View from Monbijou Bridge

TIP

● You may be tempted to "do" the Museumsinsel's five museums in one go. They are close together but each one is worth a half-day visit at least.

Berlin's famed collection of antiquities is one of the city's major treasures. To see it, head for Museums Island in the Spree. The Pergamonmusuem is one of five superb institutions here.

Altes Museum Built in 1830, this was the first museum on the island. Karl Schinkel's magnificent classical temple shares with the Pergamonmuseum (▷ 81) fabulous collections of sculptures from all corners of the ancient world. The impression made by the facade is overwhelming in itself, and hidden at the core of the building is a rotunda inspired by Rome's Pantheon and lined with statues of the gods.

Neues Museum This museum, designed in 1843 by August Stüler and sensitively restored at the turn of the 21st century, now houses Berlin's famed Ägyptisches Museum (Egyptian

Clockwise from far left: the Heyl Aphrodite, from the 2nd century BC, in the Altes Museum (Old Museum); the Altes Museum facade; a highlight of the Egyptian Museum is the bust of Queen Nefertiti; Bode-Museum exterior; Alte Nationalgalerie (Old National Gallery); rotunda in the Altes Museum, lined with antique sculptures

Museum). This rich collection of 2,000 ancient masterpieces spans three millennia. The highlight here is the bust of Queen Nefertiti, wife of Pharaoh Akhenaton. Dating from about 1340BC, the bust, made of limestone and plaster, was discovered in 1912 along with other royal portraits. Another highlight is the Temple Gate of Kalabsha, built by the Roman Emperor Augustus in 20BC.

Bode-Museum Named after Wilhelm von Bode (1845–1929), who for 20 years was curator of Museums Island, this 1904 building exhibits exquisite medieval sculptures and early Christian and Byzantine art.

Alte Nationalgalerie This gallery displays mainly 19th-century paintings, including works by Impressionists such as Manet, Monet, Renoir and Degas.

THE BASICS

smb.museum

✚ K4, K5, L5

✉ Museumsinsel

☎ 030 20 90 55 77

🕐 Tue–Wed, Fri–Sun 10–6, Thu 10–8

🚉 S-Bahn Hackescher Markt, U- and S-Bahn Friedrichstrasse

🚌 100, 200, TXL

♿ Few

💲 Moderate

Nikolaiviertel

Bronze statues (left) and period houses (right) complement this historic quarter

THE BASICS

stadtmuseum.de

🔟 L5

✉ Poststrasse

☎ Nikolaikirche and Knoblauchhaus: 030 24 00 21 62

🕐 Nikolaikirche and Knoblauchhaus: daily 10–6; Ephraim-Palais: Tue, Thu–Sun 10–6, Wed 12–8

Ⓤ U- and S-Bahn Alexanderplatz

🚌 100, 200, TXL

♿ All: moderate

HIGHLIGHTS

Nikolaikirche
● Exhibition of local history
● Gothic nave
● *The Good Samaritan*, Michael Ribestein
● Hunger Cloth (in vestry)
● Wooden *Crucifixion* of 1485

TIP

● The Nikolaikirche has weekly concerts on Fridays at 5pm (30 minutes).

Enjoy a wander through the Nikolai Quarter, a diverting pastiche of baroque and neoclassical architecture, with rows of gabled houses, cobbled streets and quaint shops.

Nikolaikirche The dominating landmark is the twin-spired church that gives the Nikolaiviertel its name. The Nikolaikirche is the oldest church in Berlin, dating from 1200 although the present building was not completed until 1470. Seriously damaged in World War II, the beautifully proportioned Gothic nave has been sensitively restored. It was here, in 1307, that the two communities of Berlin and Cölln were formally united. The church now houses a museum of local history.

Around the Quarter Two other notable buildings recall the lavish lifestyle of imperial Berlin. The pink stuccoed Knoblauchhaus was designed in 1759 by Friedrich Wilhelm Dietrichs for one of Berlin's most distinguished families. The extravagant Ephraim-Palais, with golden balconies and stone cherubs, belonged to Frederick the Great's banker, Nathan Ephraim. The interior is decorated with 17th- to 19th-century art.

Back in time Perhaps the most picturesque streets are Eiergasse and Am Nussbaum, named for its cheery reconstruction of a famous 16th-century Berlin inn, Zum Nussbaum ("At the Nut Tree")—a good refreshment stop (▷ 86).

The Pergamon Altar (left); wall design in the Aleppo Room (middle); the Ishtar Gate (right)

If you have time to visit only one museum in Berlin, choose the Pergamon. Virtually every corner of the ancient world is represented, from the Roman Empire to the Islamic world.

Controversy Like the other museums on Museums Island (▷ 78–79), the Pergamon was built to house the vast haul of antiquities amassed by German archaeologists in the 19th century. Controversy rages over the proper home for such relics; some people argue that they were wrongfully plundered. Restoration of the museum began in 2008 and is ongoing.

Pergamon Altar The museum's most stunning exhibit is the Pergamon Altar from Asia Minor, a stupendous monument so huge that it needs a hall more than 15m (50ft) high to accommodate it. From Bergama on the west coast of Turkey, it was excavated by Carl Humann in 1878–86. Dating from about 164BC, it was part of a complex of royal palaces, temples, a library and a theater. Hardly less impressive are the reconstructed market gateway of Miletus in Turkey, built by the Romans in AD120, and the Ishtar Gate from Babylon.

Antiquities The museum also has a splendid collection of Greek and Roman statues (some of them retaining traces of their original vibrant colors), Islamic art, figurines and clay tablets. Many more objects come from Sumeria and other parts of the Middle East.

THE BASICS

smb.museum

➕ K4

✉ Bodestrasse, Museumsinsel

☎ 030 266 42 42 42

🕐 Mon–Sun 10–6, Thu 10–8. Pergamon Altar to be exhibited again in 2023; long lines possible

🍽 Café

🚇 S-Bahn Hackescher Markt; U- and S-Bahn Friedrichstrasse

🚌 100, 200, TXL

💷 Expensive

HIGHLIGHTS

● 120m (394ft) frieze on Pergamon Altar
● Market gate from Miletus
● Ishtar Gate
● Facade of Mshatta Palace
● Nebuchadnezzar's throne room
● Figurines from Jericho
● Panel room from Aleppo
● Bust of the Emperor Caracalla
● Statue of Aphrodite from Myrina

More to See

DDR MUSEUM
ddr-museum.de
Step into a vanished world at this very popular interactive museum, which portrays everyday life in the Communist German Democratic Republic (East Germany). Sit in a genuine Trabbi (Trabant car), try out a typical prison cell and imagine life in a high-rise apartment block.
🚇 L5 ✉ Karl-Liebknecht-Strasse 1 ☎ 030 84 71 23 731 🕐 Sun–Fri 10–8, Sat 10–10 🚊 S-Bahn Hackescher Markt 💵 Moderate (cheaper if tickets bought online)

HUMBOLDT FORUM
humboldtforum.com
Due to open at the end of 2019, this huge new exhibition space designed by Italian architect Frank Stella will be dedicated to world culture. While the interior is entirely modern, its facade will be an exact replica of the building's predecessor, the 17th-century Stadtschloss (City Palace).
🚇 L5 ✉ Unter den Linden 3 ☎ 030 26 59 50 209 🚊 U-Bahn Hausvogteiplatz

MARX-ENGELS-DENKMAL
The two founders of Communism stand shoulder to shoulder as bronze sculptures in a garden near Alexanderplatz.
🚇 L5 ✉ Rathausstrasse 🚊 U-Bahn Alexanderplatz

MONBIJOUPARK
This leafy park by the River Spree near Museums Island has a playground and a splash pool for toddlers.
🚇 K4 ✉ Oranienburger Strasse 🚊 S-Bahn Hackescher Markt

MUSEUM THE KENNEDYS
thekennedys.de
This intriguing collection of photographs, documents, memorabilia and artifacts petaining to President John F. Kennedy's personal and family associations with Berlin includes the notes for his famous anticommunist "Ich bin ein Berliner" address at Schöneberg town hall in June 1963. There are also special exhibitions.

Marx and Engels Monument, Rathausstrasse

The DDR Museum

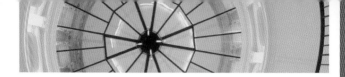

➕ K3 ✉ Auguststrasse 11–13 ☎ 030 20 65 35 70 🕐 Tue–Fri 10–6, Sat–Sun 11–6 🚇 U-Bahn Rosenthaler Strasse 🎫 Inexpensive

NEUE SYNAGOGE
cjudaicum.de

The stunning dome of the 1866 New Synagogue is a Berlin landmark. Designed by Eduard Knoblauch and August Stüler, it was destroyed during World War II. Rebuilding was completed in 1995.

➕ K4 ✉ Oranienburger Strasse 28–30 ☎ 030 88 02 83 00 🕐 Exhibitions: Apr–Sep Mon–Fri 10–6, Sun 10–7; Oct–Mar Sun–Thu 10–6, Fri 10–3 🚇 S-Bahn Oranienburger Strasse 🎫 Moderate

ROTES RATHAUS

The mid-19th-century Berlin town hall is known as the Rotes (red) Rathaus for its red brick walls. The impressive clock tower in the center is 74m (243ft) high.

➕ L5 ✉ Rathausstrasse 15 ☎ 030 902 60 🕐 Mon–Fri 9–6 🚇 U- and S-Bahn Alexanderplatz 🎫 Free

SCHLOSSBRÜCKE

Karl Friedrich Schinkel designed a new bridge to replace the old Hundebrücke in 1819. The attractive three-arched bridge is decorated with classical statues.

➕ K5 ✉ Unter den Linden 🚇 U-Bahn Hausvogteiplatz

SEA LIFE BERLIN
visitsealife.de

Ride the glass elevator through the middle of this cylindrical domed aquarium and travel into an amazing underwater world full of tropical fish.

➕ L5 ✉ Spandauer Strasse 3 ☎ 0180 66 66 90 101 🕐 Daily 10–7 🚇 S-Bahn Hackescher Markt 🎫 Expensive

SOPHIENKIRCHE
sophien.de

Berlin's sole surviving baroque church, completed in 1734, was designed by J. F. Grael.

➕ L4 ✉ Grosse Hamburger Strasse 29 ☎ 030 308 79 20 🕐 Mon–Sat 1–6; Sun before and after services 🚇 S-Bahn Hackescher Markt

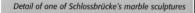

Detail of one of Schlossbrücke's marble sculptures

Schlossbrücke marks the eastern end of Unter den Linden

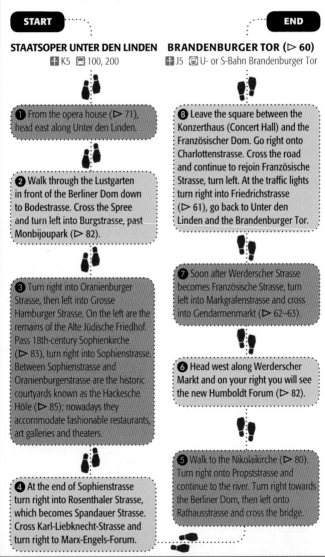

Berlin Mitte

This walk heads through a part of town that was once at the heart of the former East Berlin.

DISTANCE: 5km (3.1 miles) **ALLOW:** 2 hours

START

STAATSOPER UNTER DEN LINDEN
🔲 K5 🚌 100, 200

END

BRANDENBURGER TOR (▷ 60)
🔲 J5 🚇 U- or S-Bahn Brandenburger Tor

① From the opera house (▷ 71), head east along Unter den Linden.

② Walk through the Lustgarten in front of the Berliner Dom down to Bodestrasse. Cross the Spree and turn left into Burgstrasse, past Monbijoupark (▷ 82).

③ Turn right into Oranienburger Strasse, then left into Grosse Hamburger Strasse. On the left are the remains of the Alte Jüdische Friedhof. Pass 18th-century Sophienkirche (▷ 83), turn right into Sophienstrasse. Between Sophienstrasse and Oranienburgerstrasse are the historic courtyards known as the Hackesche Höfe (▷ 85); nowadays they accommodate fashionable restaurants, art galleries and theaters.

④ At the end of Sophienstrasse turn right into Rosenthaler Strasse, which becomes Spandauer Strasse. Cross Karl-Liebknecht-Strasse and turn right to Marx-Engels-Forum.

⑧ Leave the square between the Konzerthaus (Concert Hall) and the Französischer Dom. Go right onto Charlottenstrasse. Cross the road and continue to rejoin Französische Strasse, turn left. At the traffic lights turn right into Friedrichstrasse (▷ 61), go back to Unter den Linden and the Brandenburger Tor.

⑦ Soon after Werderscher Strasse becomes Französische Strasse, turn left into Markgrafenstrasse and cross into Gendarmenmarkt (▷ 62–63).

⑥ Head west along Werderscher Markt and on your right you will see the new Humboldt Forum (▷ 82).

⑤ Walk to the Nikolaikirche (▷ 80). Turn right onto Propststrasse and continue to the river. Turn right towards the Berliner Dom, then left onto Rathausstrasse and cross the bridge.

Shopping

AMPELMANN SHOP

ampelmann.de

Named for the little man on pedestrian traffic lights, this shop is the place to go for Berlin bears and other souvenirs.

➕ L5 ✉ Karl-Liebknecht-Strasse 5 ☎ 030 84 71 20 45 Ⓢ S-Bahn Hackescher Markt

ERZGEBIRGSKUNST ORIGINAL

dregeno.de

Traditional Christmas decorations beautifully crafted from wood are a great souvenir from Germany.

➕ L4 ✉ Sophienstrasse 9 ☎ 030 28 04 51 30 Ⓤ U-Bahn Weinmeisterstrasse

HACKESCHE HÖFE

hackesche-hoefe.com

These eight historic art nouveau courtyards are at the forefront of Berlin's art scene with art galleries, workshops, boutiques, cafés and entertainment venues.

➕ L4 ✉ Rosenthaler Strasse 40–41 Ⓢ S-Bahn Hackescher Markt

NIX

nix.de

Nix sells a sophisticated range of fashion clothing for all the family.

➕ K4 ✉ Heckmann Höfe, Oranienburger Strasse 32 ☎ 030 281 80 44 Ⓢ S-Bahn Oranienburger Strasse

R.S.V.P. PAPER

rsvp-berlin.de

This colorful shop sells calendars, greeting cards, wrapping paper and everything you need to write a letter.

➕ L4 ✉ Mulackstrasse 14 & 26 ☎ 030 31 95 64 Ⓤ U-Bahn Rosenthaler Platz

Entertainment and Nightlife

B-FLAT

b-flat-berlin.de

Listen to acoustic music and jazz at this downtown club. Specially designed for this genre of music, the acoustics and atmosphere are unparalleled and the club is popular with the big names in jazz. There is an entrance charge, but drinks are cheaper before 10pm.

➕ L3 ✉ Dirckenstrasse 40 ☎ 030 283 11 23 🕐 Mon–Sat 8pm–late Ⓤ U-Bahn Weinmeisterstrasse

CHAMÄLEON

chamaeleonberlin.com

You don't need to understand German to access the hard-to-categorize fusion shows put on at this variety theater—a mix of music, dance, mime, comedy, acrobatics and more, which the theater calls "New Circus".

➕ L4 ✉ Hackesche Höfe, Rosenthaler Strasse 40–41 ☎ 030 40 00 590 🕐 Shows nightly at 8pm Ⓢ S-Bahn Hackescher Markt

KINO BABYLON

babylonberlin.eu

This 1929 art deco cinema has had its organ restored to provide the "soundtrack" the directors of old silent films intended. It also shows a wide range of modern films, including some in original language.

➕ L4 ✉ Rosa-Luxemburg-Strasse 30 ☎ 030 242 59 69 🕐 Mon–Sat 12–late, Sun 6pm–late Ⓤ U-Bahn Rosa-Luxemburg-Platz

Where to Eat

PRICES

Prices are approximate, based on a 3-course meal for one person.

€€€ over €40
€€ €20–€40
€ up to €20

ACHT&DREISSIG (€€)

restaurant38berlin.de

German classics with seasonal twists are presented as tapas-style tasters here. The homemade egg noodles (*Spätzle*) are particularly good.

🔲 K4 ✉ Oranienburger Strasse 38 ☎ 030 37 46 50 31 🕐 Mon–Fri 12–11, Sat 5–11 🚇 U-Bahn Oranienburger Tor

HACKESCHER HOF (€€)

hackescher-hof.de

A restaurant-café-wine bar with an old-fashioned appeal and a locally sourced menu of European cuisine.

🔲 L4 ✉ Rosenthaler Strasse 40–41 ☎ 030 283 52 93 🕐 Mon–Fri 8am–3am, Sat–Sun 9am–3am 🚇 S-Bahn Hackescher Markt

LOKAL (€€)

lokal-berlin.blogspot.com

This small restaurant, with a modern, homey atmosphere, serves modern European cuisine with beautifully presented vegetarian options.

🔲 K4 ✉ Linienstrasse 160 ☎ 030 28 44 95 00 🕐 Daily 5–11 🚇 U-Bahn Oranienburger Tor

MONSIEUR VUONG (€)

monsieurvuong.de

For a complete change, come here for delicious Vietnamese dishes. The menu changes every other day.

🔲 L4 ✉ Alte Schönhauser Strasse 46 ☎ 030 99 29 69 24 🕐 Mon–Thu 12–11pm, Fri–Sun 12–midnight 🚇 U-Bahn Weinmeisterstrasse

OSSENA (€–€€)

ossena.de

Popular with visitors and locals alike for its warm welcome and prompt service, Ossena serves excellent Italian cuisine.

🔲 L4 ✉ Neue Promenade 6 ☎ 030 24 08 86 67 🕐 9am–1am 🚇 S-Bahn Hackescher Markt

OXYMORON (€€)

oxymoron-berlin.de

Find delicious Italian and French food at this 1920s-style restaurant in Hackesche Höfe; it also has a stylish lounge bar and dance floor.

🔲 L4 ✉ Hackesche Höfe, Rosenthaler Strasse 40–41 ☎ 030 28 39 18 86 🕐 Daily 9am–1am 🚇 S-Bahn Hackescher Markt

SIXTIES (€)

sixtiesdiner.de

Red, white and blue are the signature colors of this brash 1960s American diner that rustles up pretty decent burgers and fries, steaks, tacos and more.

🔲 K4 ✉ Oranienburger Strasse 11 ☎ 030 28 59 90 41 🕐 Sun–Thu 10am–2am, Fri–Sat 10am–4am 🚇 S-Bahn Hackescher Markt

TRATTORIA PIAZZA ROSSA (€€)

piazza-rossa.com

Smartly dressed folk meet at this eatery in the Rathaus Passagen for Italian fish and meat dishes and great pizzas.

🔲 L5 ✉ Rathausstrasse 13 ☎ 030 612 24 29 🕐 Daily 11am–midnight 🚇 U- and S-Bahn Alexanderplatz

ZUM NUSSBAUM (€)

The Nut Tree is an artful re-creation of Berlin's oldest tavern. It serves traditional German cuisine, but the real draw is the great selection of beers.

🔲 L5 ✉ Am Nussbaum 3 ☎ 030 242 30 95 🕐 Daily 12–12 🚇 U-Bahn Klosterstrasse

Prenzlauer Berg

Once a solidly blue-collar neighborhood, Prenzlauer Berg been thoroughly gentrified, and the immaculate apartment blocks are now inhabited largely by upwardly mobile young professionals and their families. The numerous bars, cafés, restaurants and boutiques reflect this change.

Top 25

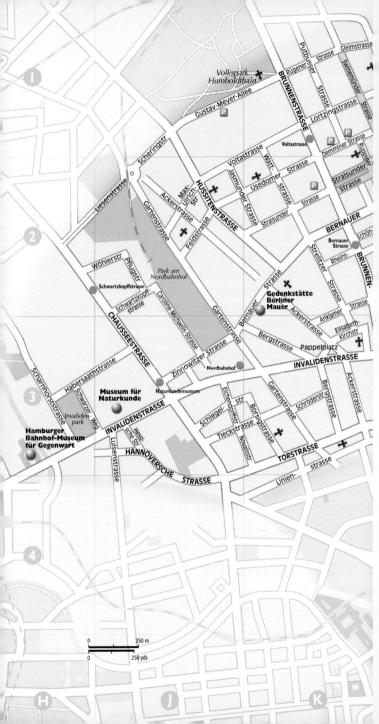

Gedenkstätte Berliner Mauer

To really understand what is was like for Berliners to live in the shadow of the Berlin Wall, visit this ambitious memorial commemorating the individuals who perished trying to cross the notorious "death strip" to freedom.

Bernauer Strasse The open-air site extends some 1.4km (0.9 miles) along Bernauer Strasse, from Nordbahnhof station to the Mauerpark (▷ 94) along the former border strip separating East and West Berlin. It incorporates a 400m-long (1,300ft) section of the original wall. The space in between the concrete wall and another fence, 100m farther into the East German side, became known as the death strip, as most attempts to cross it proved fatal. The section here has been grassed over

Clockwise from far left: the Chapel of Reconciliation with its striking wooden slat exterior; iron poles mark the route of the wall, with an intact section of the concrete wall left in the middle; the Documentation Center has displays on the history of the Wall

Gedenkstätte Berliner Mauer
Berlin Wall Memorial

and is used to illustrate the tragic effect of the wall on family members, friends and neighbors who overnight found themselves separated, a situation that was to persist for 28 long years (1961–89). You can see the immediate impact on the residents of Bernauer Strasse by watching the 20-minute documentary film in the visitor center. Another short film illustrated the lengths to which the East German authorities were prepared to go to deter would-be defectors: guard dogs, barbed wire, machine-gun posts, electrified fences and tank traps.

Documentation Center The exhibitions here explain the background: how the wall came to be, why it fell and what followed. When you have finished here,, venture onto the parapet for panoramic views across no man's land.

THE BASICS

berliner-mauer-
gedenkstaette.de

⊞ K2

✉ Bernauer Strasse 111

☎ 030 46 79 86 666

🕐 Tue–Sun 10–6

🚊 S-Bahn Nordbahnhof,
U-Bahn Bernauer Strasse

🚌 245, 246, tram M10

🍴 Café and bistros

♿ Free

Husemannstrasse

TOP 25

Cafés have sprung up along the charming, tree-lined Husemannstrasse

THE BASICS

🚊 M2
✉ Prenzlauer Berg
🚇 U-Bahn Eberswalder Strasse
🚋 Tram M1, M10, M12
🍴 Many ethnic restaurants and cafés

HIGHLIGHTS

● Prater Biergarten (beer garden)
● KulturBrauerei
● Museum in der KulturBrauerei (▷ 95)

This area just north of Kollwitzplatz is typical of the transformation Prenzlauer Berg has undergone in recent years. Don't miss the many cultural attractions in the converted KulturBrauerei.

Cultured place Husemannstrasse stands at the heart of the action in Prenzlauer Berg, where fashionable stores and cafés have taken over the ground floor areas of renovated postwar apartment blocks. Among the small-scale cultural foundations in this area are the Theater o.N. (Zinnober), founded as the first free theater of the German Democratic Republic (Kollwitzstrasse 53), and the Prater theater in Kastanienallee, which boasts the oldest beer garden in Berlin (▷ 96). However, the undoubted star of the show is the KulturBrauerei (▷ 95), a multifunctional cultural complex that occupies the handsome buildings of a massive former brewery. It includes theaters, performance and practice venues for alternative music and theater groups, a cinema multiplex, restaurants, and the East German commercial design collection of the Museum in der KulturBrauerei (▷ 94).

Going north At the north end of Husemannstrasse, Danziger Strasse connects with the busy traffic intersection outside the Eberswalder Strasse U-Bahn station. This is on the way to north Prenzlauer Berg (more residential) and Pankow, and to the sports facilities at the Friedrich-Ludwig-Jahn-Sportpark.

Kollwitzplatz

Gustav Seitz's statue of Käthe Kollwitz sits at the heart of the square

This much-loved leafy square in the heart of Prenzlauer Berg is named after the artist Käthe Kollwitz (1867–1945). Overlooking the pretty landscaped garden are sidewalk cafés, bars and restaurants.

On the up For many years Käthe Kollwitz lived nearby on what is now Kollwitzstrasse. The square's centerpiece is a bronze memorial sculpture by Gustav Seitz (1961). The handsome apartment buildings around it were constructed during the Grundeszeit, the period following German unification in 1871. During the Battle for Berlin in 1945, most houses suffered severe bomb damage and for a long time afterward bullet and shrapnel holes pitted the facades. Since the late 1990s there has been a complete transformation so that now only the wealthy (mostly young professionals) can afford to live here. There's a Saturday market where you can buy organic fruit, vegetables and eggs.

Jewish character South of Kollwitzplatz, in Rykestrasse, stands the Jüdische Schule (1904), a large former Jewish school, which now houses a synagogue and a Jewish educational foundation. Nearby, the grounds of what was once a Jewish cemetery have been taken over by a playground and a housing and office development. Across the way, a massive *Wasserturm* (water tower) in a small park is a signature image of the area. Close to where Knaackstrasse emerges into Prenzlauer Allee is the Museum Pankow (▷ 94), about local life.

THE BASICS

✚ M2
✉ Prenzlauer Berg
🚇 U-Bahn Eberswalder Strasse, Senefelderplatz
🚋 Tram M1, M10, M12
🍴 Many ethnic restaurants and cafés

HIGHLIGHTS

● Jüdische Schule
● Wasserturm
● Käthe Kollwitz sculpture
● Museum Pankow
(▷ 94)

PRENZLAUER BERG TOP 25

More to See

HAMBURGER BAHNHOF-MUSEUM FÜR GEGENWART

smb.museum

This huge exhibition space in a renovated former railway station specializes in contemporary art from around the world, from painting and sculpture to immersive art.

🚉 H3 ✉ Invalidenstrasse 50–51 ☎ 030 39 78 34 12 🕐 Tue, Wed, Fri 10–6, Thu 10–8, Sat 11–6, Sun 11–6 🚇 S- and U-Bahn Hauptbahnhof 💶 Moderate

MAUERPARK

mauerpark.info

Occupying the former border strip, this green space hosts all kinds of social events, from a Sunday flea market to concerts, exhibitions and karaoke nights in the amphitheater.

🚉 L1 ✉ Eberswalder Strasse 🚇 U-Bahn Eberswalder Strasse 🚊 Tram M10

MUSEUM IN DER KULTURBRAUEREI

hdg.de

The exhibition "Everyday Life in Communist East Germany" focuses on the impact of political constraints on design, from cars and furniture to everyday objects, such as matchboxes, magazines and soap bars.

🚉 M2 ✉ Knaackstrasse 97 ☎ 030 473 77 79 40 🕐 Tue–Fri 9–7, Sat–Sun 10–6 🚇 U-Bahn Eberswalder Strasse 💶 Inexpensive

MUSEUM FÜR NATURKUNDE

naturkundemuseum-berlin.de

The Natural History Museum has the world's largest dinosaur skeleton as well as a vast collection of geological and zoological exhibits.

🚉 J3 ✉ Invalidenstrasse 43 ☎ 030 88 91 40 🕐 Tue–Fri 9.30–6, Sat–Sun 10–6 🚇 U-Bahn Naturkundemuseum 💶 Moderate

MUSEUM PANKOW

This local museum focuses on life here between 1949 and 1990, before gentrification took hold.

🚉 M3 ✉ Prenzlauer Allee 227–228 ☎ 030 902 95 39 17 🕐 Mon–Fri 9–7 🚇 U-Bahn Senefelderplatz 🚊 Tram M2 💶 Free

Karaoke session in the Mauerpark

Shopping

DA CAPO

da-capo-vinyl.de

This small record shop is packed with vinyl—mainly jazz, soul and 60s rock, but you will also find music from the former GDR.

🚇 M2 ✉ Kastanienallee 962 ☎ 030 448 17 71 🚇 U-Bahn Eberswalder Strasse

GURU-SHOP

guru-shop.de

Guru is filled with exotic goods from India, Nepal, Thailand and North Africa, including beautiful printed textiles, banana-leaf notebooks, jewelry and recycled paper products.

🚇 M1 ✉ Pappelallee 2 ☎ 030 44 01 33 72 🚇 U-Bahn Eberswalder Strasse

MR & MRS PEPPERS

mrandmrspeppers.de

This is the place to shop for 1970s-style clothing for men and women, made from fabrics printed to their own design. There's also antique clothing, including bathing suits.

🚇 L2 ✉ Kastanienallee 91–92 ☎ 030 448 11 21 🚇 U-Bahn Eberswalder Strasse

TAUSCHE

tausche.de

Tausche has a range of fun bags and rucksacks for men and women. You get two different flaps with each bag—just zip on the one that fits your mood.

🚇 M1 ✉ Raumerstrasse 8 ☎ 030 40 30 17 70 🚇 U-Bahn Eberswalder Strasse

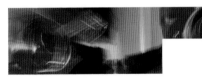

Entertainment and Nightlife

BADFISH

This highly rated bar-hangout has frozen margaritas, a long whisky menu and live music.

🚇 M1 ✉ Stargarerstrasse 13 ☎ 030 54 71 47 88 🕐 Daily 5pm–5am 🚇 S-Bahn Prenzlauer Allee

KESSELHAUS

knesselhaus.net

Enjoy dance nights in a converted brewery boiler house. This buzzing place hosts international and German bands.

🚇 M2 ✉ Knaackstrasse 97 ☎ 030 44 31 50 🕐 From 8pm 🚇 U-Bahn Eberswalder Strasse

KULTURBRAUEREI

kulturbrauerei-berlin.de

The great brick buildings of the former former Schultheiss brewery are now a multipurpose nightlife, entertainment and dining venue. Here you'll find SODA, one of Berlin's biggest clubs, and Frannz (▷ 96), with its comfortable TV lounge. The CineStar cinema has eight auditoriums and some OV (original version) films. Expect crowds on weekends.

🚇 M2 ✉ Schönhauser Allee 36 ☎ 030 44 31 51 55 🕐 Times vary 🚇 U-Bahn Eberswalder Strasse

LYRIK

cafe-lyrik.de

An informal music club with an intimate feel, this café offers a changing program that ranges from chansons to tango, klezmer or gypsy jazz.

🚇 M2 ✉ Kollwitzstrasse 97 ☎ 030 44 31 71 91 🕐 Concerts Wed–Sat 🚇 U-Bahn Eberswalder Strasse

Where to Eat

PRICES

Prices are approximate, based on a 3-course meal for one person.

€€€ over €40
€€   €20–€40
€   up to €20

FRANNZ (€€)

Housed in the KulturBrauerei cultural complex, Frannz offers fusion cuisine in a room fitted out in a cool modern style, or on an outside terrace in summer. There's also a beer garden.

🔢 M2 ✉ Schönhauser Allee 36 ☎ 030 726 27 93 60 🕐 Thu–Sun 6pm–late 🚇 U-Bahn Eberswalder Strasse

KONNOPKE'S IMBISS (€)

konnopke-imbiss.de

If you are a fan of that Berlin delicacy, *Currywurst* (sausage with a curry-ketchup sauce) with fries, there's no better place than at this fashionable snackbar under the U-Bahn station.

🔢 M2 ✉ Schönhauser Allee 44a ☎ 030 442 77 65 🕐 Mon–Fri 10am–8pm, Sat 12–8, Sun 12–6 🚇 U-Bahn Eberswalder Strasse

MAO THAI STAMMHAUS (€€)

maothai.de

Tuck into classic Thai fare in East Berlin's first (and best) Thai restaurant. The exquisitely presented dishes are accompanied by edible vegetable decorations.

🔢 M2 ✉ Wörther Strasse 30 ☎ 030 441 92 61 🕐 Daily 12–11.30pm 🚇 U-Bahn Senefelderplatz

METZER ECK (€)

metzer-eck.de

Prenzlauer Berg's oldest eatery opened in 1913 and little has changed since. The traditional *Kneipe* fare is served on small plates and no dish is over €10.

🔢 M3 ✉ Metzer Strasse 33 ☎ 030 442 76 56 🕐 Mon–Fri 4pm–1am, Sat 6pm–1am 🚇 U-Bahn Senefelderplatz

NEUGRÜNS KÖCHE (€€)

neugruenskoeche.de

This relaxed restaurant offers two alternating seven-course menus—Mediterranean or regional.

🔢 M1 ✉ Schönhauser Allee 135a ☎ 030 44 01 20 92 🕐 Wed–Sat 7pm–midnight 🚇 U-Bahn Eberswalder Strasse

PASTERNAK (€€)

restaurant-pasternak.de

Marina Lehmann's lovely restaurant, which serves a wide range of traditional Russo-Jewish fare, has a literary theme.

🔢 M2 ✉ Knaackstrasse 22–24 ☎ 030 441 33 99 🕐 Daily 9am–1am 🚇 U-Bahn Senefelderplatz

PETER-PAUL (€€)

peterpaul.berlin

If you want to sample a variety of German foods in one meal, the tapa-sized portions here are for you. Tasty choices include *Maultaschen* (vegetarian ravioli), *Bouletten* (meatballs) and *Sauerbraten* (pot roast).

🔢 L3 ✉ Torstrasse 99 ☎ 030 43 77 30 43 🕐 Mon–Sat 6pm–1am 🚇 U-Bahn Rosenthaler Platz

PRATER GARTEN (€–€€)

prater-biergarten.de

Berlin's oldest beer garden is a shady spot to try Prater beer. The on-site restaurant serves traditional fare with seasonal variations.

🔢 L2 ✉ Kastanienallee 7–9 ☎ 030 448 56 88 🕐 Restaurant: Mon–Sat from 6pm, Sun from 12pm. Garden: Apr–Sep daily 12–12, weather permitting 🚇 U-Bahn Eberswalder Strasse

Farther Afield

Berliners are spoiled for choice when it's time to get away from the stresses of city life. Brandenburg is known as the "land of 3,000 lakes," and many of the state's myriad parks, forests, lakes, castles and pretty villages are in easy reach of the city.

BERNAU

ZEPERNICK

BUCH

16

ESS
109

FRANZÖSISCH
BUCHHOLZ

SCHWANEBECK

17

KAROW
10

1

71
Peckberge

ESS

158

3

E28

158

BLANKENBURG

114

MALCHOW

4

5

WARTENBERG

109

WEISSENSEE

HÖNOW

2

HOHEN-
SCHÖNHAUSEN

MARZAHN

Zeiss-
Grossplanetarium

LICHTENBERG

FRIEDRICHS-
HAIN

1   5

KAULSDORF

East Side
Gallery

FRIEDRICHS-
FELDE

BIESDORF

Tierpark
Berlin

KARLSHORST

NEUKÖLLN

Treptower
Park

BAUMSCHULENWEG

25

FRIEDRICHS-
HAGEN

23

24

1

96a

KÖPENICK

Grosser
Müggelsee

2

JOHANNISTHAL

BRITZ

3   113

Schloss
Köpenick

Britzer
Garten

Teltowkanal

Dahme

E36

BUCKOW

179

5

GRÜNAU

RUDOW

ALT-
GLIENICKE

LICHTENRADE

6

BOHNSDORF

7

Jagdschloss Grunewald

This Renaissance-style hunting lodge has been used for more than 400 years

THE BASICS

Jagdschloss Grunewald
spsg.de
➕ See map ▷ 98
✉ Hüttenweg 100, Am Grunewaldsee
☎ 0331 969 42 22
🕐 Apr–Oct Tue–Sun 10–5.30; Nov–Mar Sat–Sun 10–4
🚉 S-Bahn Grunewald
🚌 M19, M29, X10, 115, 186, 249, 349
♿ Inexpensive

Grunewaldturm
✉ Havelchaussee 61, Wilmersdorf
☎ 030 300 07 30
🕐 Tower: daily 10–6
🍴 Restaurant
🚉 S-Bahn Grunewald
🚌 218
♿ Moderate

HIGHLIGHTS

● Hunting museum
● *Adam and Eve* and *Judith*, Lucas Cranach the Elder
● *Julius Caesar*, Rubens
● Wooden ceiling in the Great Hall

This attractive Renaissance hunting lodge was built in 1542 by Elector Joachim II of Brandenburg on the shores of Grunewaldsee for his mistress. It was untouched during World War II and is Berlin's oldest surviving palace.

Hunting lodge Originally the lodge was surrounded by a moat, but this was gradually filled in. Friedrich I introduced baroque modifications and outbuildings at the start of the 18th century and painted the facade a brilliant white. However, the Renaissance Grosser Saal (Great Hall), with its remarkable painted ceiling, remained. In true Renaissance style, Elector Joachim II commissioned many paintings from Lucas Cranach the Elder (and his son, the Younger), and these now form a permanent collection in the lodge. There are also exhibitions on hunting themes, portraits of the rulers of Brandenburg and Prussia, and works of the 17th-century Dutch school.

Grunewald forest Paths crisscross the 32sq km (12sq miles) of woodland, beaches fringe the Havel, and there is space for leisure pursuits from boating to hang-gliding. You can swim in the Grunewaldsee, the lake on which the hunting lodge stands, and, farther south, in the Krumme Lanke. Between these two lakes is a marshy nature reserve known as the Langes Luch. For views, climb the Grunewaldturm, a 72m (236ft) folly on the banks of the Havel, built in memory of Kaiser Wilhelm I in 1897.

The 16th-century Zitadelle at Spandau (left); Nikolaikirche in the Altstadt (right)

Spandauer Zitadelle

Of the many attractive villages on Berlin's outskirts, ancient Spandau, with its red-brick Zitadelle, picturesque streets and views across the Havel, stands out. The best vantage point is the Juliusturm, the oldest surviving part of the complex.

The Zitadelle A strategic location at the confluence of the rivers Spree and Havel made Spandau important in the Middle Ages. The first Zitadelle (fortress), dating from the 12th century, was rebuilt by Joachim III in 1557. Climb up to the top of the 36m-high (120ft) crenellated Juliusturm for splendid views. Most of the bastions and outbuildings date from the 19th century, though the Old Magazine is as ancient as the castle itself.

Many lives The fortress last saw active service during the Napoleonic Wars, when the Old Arsenal was reduced to ruins. Now it houses the City History Museum with everyday articles from Spandau's past. Just inside the castle gateway is the statue of a defiant Albrecht the Bear, first margrave of Brandenburg and famous for his war-mongering.

Altstadt Spandau The attractive Old Town is a short walk from the castle. The Gotisches Haus (Gothic House) in Breite Strasse dates from 1232. Reformationsplatz, the central square, has plenty of cafés and the splendid Gothic church, Nikolaikirche. North of here lies the quaint old area known as the Kolk.

THE BASICS

zitadelle-spandau.de
+ See map ▷ 98
✉ Am Juliusturm 64, Spandau
☎ 030 354 94 40
🕐 Daily 10–5
🍴 Am Juliusturm, Zitadelle
🚇 U-Bahn Zitadelle
🚌 X33
🚉 Spandau
♿ Few
💶 Inexpensive

HIGHLIGHTS

● Cannons
● Statue of Albrecht the Bear
● Museum of the Middle Ages
● Juliusturm
● Bastion walls
● Old Magazine
● Ruined arsenal
● Kolk

More to See

BOTANISCHER GARTEN

bgbm.org

See more than 18,000 varieties of plants and flowers in beautifully landscaped botanical gardens.

➕ See map ▷ 98 ✉ Königin-Luise-Strasse 6–8, Dahlem ☎ 030 83 85 01 00 ⏰ Daily 9–8 (or dusk if earlier); may vary during events Ⓢ S-Bahn Botanischer Garten 🚌 Moderate

BRITZER GARTEN

gruen-berlin.de

Created for the National Garden Show in 1985, the 100ha (247-acre) site is popular with Berliners. There are nature trails, a lake and a restaurant.

➕ See map ▷ 99 ✉ Sangerhauser Weg 1, Neukölln ☎ 030 700 90 86 ⏰ Daily 9–dusk 🚌 179 🚌 Inexpensive

BRÜCKE MUSEUM

bruecke-museum.de

This gallery exhibits work from the group of 20th-century German Expressionist artists known as Die Brücke (The Bridge).

➕ See map ▷ 98 ✉ Bussardsteig 9, Dahlem ☎ 030 831 20 29 ⏰ Wed–Mon 11–5 🚌 115 🚌 Moderate

EAST SIDE GALLERY

eastsidegallery-berlin.com

See graffiti art as displayed on 730m (2,395ft) of the former Berlin Wall, on the north bank of the River Spree. It is said to be the world's largest open-air art gallery.

➕ See map ▷ 99 ✉ Mühlenstrasse Ⓤ U- and S-Bahn Warschauer Strasse 🚌 Free

FILMPARK BABELSBERG

filmpark-babelsberg.de

The hub of Germany's film industry for 100 years, these vast studios were responsible for such classics as *Metropolis* (1927) and *The Blue Angel* (1930). You can enjoy a studio tour and experience the cinema of the future at this popular theme park.

➕ See map ▷ 98 ✉ Grossbeeren-strasse 200, 14482 Potsdam ☎ Ticket hotline: 0331 72 12 34 45 ⏰ Mid-Mar to Oct daily 10–6 🚌 Expensive 🚌 601, 619, 690 from Potsdam train station

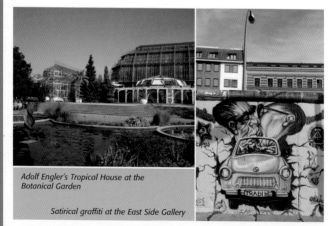

Adolf Engler's Tropical House at the Botanical Garden

Satirical graffiti at the East Side Gallery

FREIZEITPARK TEGEL

Berlin's best park for children, Tegel has table tennis, rowing, trampolines, volleyball, pedal boats and chess. Cruises depart from the Greenwich promenade nearby.

➕ See map ▷ 98 ✉ Campestrasse 11 ☎ 030 434 66 66 🕐 May–Sep daily 8–5 (attractions); park: 24 hours 🚇 U-Bahn Alt-Tegel 🎫 Free

FRIEDRICHSHAGEN

A distinct small town within the big city, this has always been a popular spot at the Müggelsee, Berlin's largest lake. In summer, it's especially popular for water sports.

➕ See map ▷ 99 ✉ Köpenick 🚈 S-Bahn Friedrichshagen 🚋 Tram 60, 61 to Seebad Friedrichshagen

GEDENKSTÄTTE HAUS DER WANNSEE KONFERENZ

ghwk.de

In this innocuous-looking mansion beside the shores of the Wannsee lake, leading Nazis plotted the deliberate and systematic mass extermination of Europe's 11 million Jews. The exhibition tells the whole horrific story.

➕ See map ▷ 98 ✉ Am Grossen Wannsee 56–58, Zehlendorf ☎ 030 805 00 10 🕐 Daily 10–6 🚈 S-Bahn Wannsee 🎫 Free

GEDENKSTÄTTE SACHSENHAUSEN

stiftung-bg.de

Some 100,000 prisoners perished at this concentration camp during World War II. The great lie "Work makes you free," inscribed on the entrance gate, is a chilling reminder of the deception and evil once perpetrated here. Two museums tell the terrible story of the camp. One focuses on the plight of the Jews; the other, in the former kitchens, focuses on the daily life of the inmates.

➕ See map ▷ 98 ✉ Strasse der Nationen 22 ☎ 033 01 20 02 00 🕐 Mid-Mar to mid-Oct daily 8.30–6; mid-Oct to mid-Mar 8.30–4.30 🚈 S-Bahn Oranienburg (then 20-minute walk) 🚉 Oranienburg 🚻 Few 🎫 Free

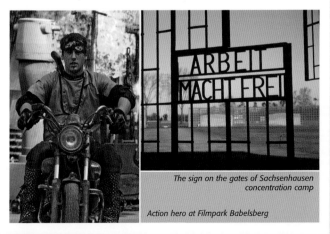

The sign on the gates of Sachsenhausen concentration camp

Action hero at Filmpark Babelsberg

MUSEUMSDORF DÜPPEL

dueppel.de

On the site of a village founded around 1170, this open-air living museum is a re-creation of a medieval village. Costumed actors provide an insight into life in the Berlin area during the Middle Ages.

🔛 See map ▷ 98 ✉ Clauerstrasse 11, Zehlendorf ☎ 030 802 66 71 🕐 Sun and hols 10–5, Thu 3–7 🚇 S-Bahn Mexikoplatz, then bus 118 🎫 Inexpensive

OLYMPIASTADION

olympiastadion-berlin.de

The Olympic Stadium was built to host the 1936 Olympic Games, but it was remodeled in 2006 for the final of another major sporting event, the soccer World Cup. Features of the original were preserved, including some of the heroic sculptures and stelae and the original bell from the Glockenturm (bell tower).

🔛 See map ▷ 98 ✉ Olympischer Platz 3 ☎ 030 25 00 23 22 (information); 030 68 81 00 (stadium) 🚇 U- and S-Bahn Olympiastadion 🎫 Expensive

SCHLOSS KÖPENICK

smb.museum

Standing in peaceful parkland, this elegant 17th-century palace houses a museum of decorative arts.

🔛 See map ▷ 99 ✉ Schlossinsel, Köpenick ☎ 030 266 42 42 42 🕐 Tue–Sun 11–6 🍴 Café 🚇 S-Bahn Spindlersfeld 🚌 164, 167; tram 27, 60, 61, 62, 67 🎫 Inexpensive

TIERPARK BERLIN

tierpark.berlin.de

One of Berlin's two zoos, Tierpark, on the east side of the city, is in grounds that once formed part of Schloss Friedrichsfelde. Events are held in the restored palace.

🔛 See map ▷ 99 ✉ Am Tierpark 125 ☎ 030 51 53 10 🕐 Jan–mid Mar and Nov–Dec daily 9–4; mid-Sep to Oct daily 9–5; mid-Mar–mid-Sep daily 9–6 🚇 U-Bahn Tierpark 🚌 296, 396; tram 27, 37 🎫 Expensive

TREPTOWER PARK

The largest green space on the eastern side of the city spreads out along the banks of the River Spree. Fairs and other events are often held here.

🔛 See map ▷ 99 ✉ Puschkinallee 🚇 S-Bahn Treptower Park

VOLKSPARK JUNGFERNHEIDE

This large park, on the northern edge of Charlottenburg, offers swimming, boat rental, hiking, sports fields and a theater.

🔛 See map ▷ 98 ✉ Saatwinkler Damm 🚇 U-Bahn Jakob-Kaiser-Platz

WANNSEE FÄHRE

The enjoyable ferry ride from Wannsee to Kladow is inexpensive (free with a BVG *Tageskarte* or AB single ticket, *Einzelfarschein*). The ride takes 20 minutes and departures are hourly.

🔛 See map ▷ 98 ✉ Wannsee Pier ⛴ Ferry F10 🚇 U-Bahn Wannsee

ZEISS-GROSSPLANETARIUM

planetarium.berlin

Built during the 1980s to match a planetarium in West Berlin, this uses the latest optical and laser technology for its astronomy shows.

🔛 See map ▷ 99 ✉ Prenzlauer Allee 80 ☎ 030 421 84 10 🕐 Shows daily 2 and 4pm and varying additional times 🚇 S-Bahn Prenzlauer Allee 🎫 Moderate

Excursion: Potsdam

ALTER MARKT

Potsdam, the capital of the state of Brandenburg, lies 24km (15 miles) southwest of Berlin. Its hub is the Old Market, with the neoclassical Nikolaikirche, the last work of Karl Friedrich Schinkel, at its heart. King Friedrich Wilhelm IV commissioned the building when he was crown prince, but he had to wait until after his father died before completing the project and adding the distinctive dome to the roof. On the eastern side of the square, the 18th-century baroque Altes Rathaus (Old City Hall), adorned with a gilded figure of Atlas, forms part of Potsdam's city walls. Framing the remaining sides of the square is the Stadtschloss, destroyed during World War II but largely reconstructed in 2007–13 to house the Brandenburg regional parliament.

SANSSOUCI

spsg.de

On the western edge of Potsdam you'll find landscaped Sanssouci Park, a UNESCO World Heritage Site. It contains two quite different yet equally impressive palaces built for Frederick the Great. Formal gardens, terraces lined with fruit trees, fountains and follies complete the picture. Schloss Sanssouci (the name means "without a care") was designed by Georg Wenzeslaus von Knobelsdorff as Frederick's summer palace and completed in 1747. The single-story rococo facade, topped by a shallow green dome, conceals a succession of gorgeously furnished rooms and a charming collection of precious objects. Frederick loved to stay here with his friends, and is buried on the highest terrace on the hill.

The New Palace (Neues Palais), with its three-story redbrick facade and massive dome, is a complete contrast. Completed in 1769, it was intended to impress. The sumptuous interior was designed by Karl von Gontard. About a dozen of the palace's 200 or so rooms are open to visitors, including the Marble Hall and the Grotto Hall, with its precious-stone-encrusted walls.

Excursion: Potsdam

THE BASICS

✉ Im Neuen Garten 11
☎ 0331 969 42 00
🕐 Apr–Oct Tue–Sun 10–5.30; Nov–Mar Tue–Sun 10–4.30
🍴 Restaurant
🚉 S-Bahn Potsdam Hauptbahnhof
🚌 692
💶 Moderate

SCHLOSS CECILIENHOF

spsg.de

Set in parkland north of Potsdam is Schloss Cecilienhof, built for Crown Prince Wilhelm, Kaiser Wilhelm II's son, and his wife, Cecilie. Completed in 1917, it is an early 20th-century reproduction of a half-timbered English Tudor manor house, arranged around a succession of courtyards and finished with 55 different decorative brick chimney stacks. The palace fit perfectly into the surrounding English-style garden. The Hohenzollerns were able to continue living here even after the abolition of the monarchy in 1918, but after World War II the palace was seized by the Soviets. In the summer of 1945, US president Harry S. Truman, Soviet political leader Joseph Stalin and British prime minister Winston Churchill met here for the Potsdam Conference to shape the fate of the postwar world. Cecilienhof is now a luxury hotel but the conference rooms are open to the public, and you can see the crown prince and princess's apartments on a guided tour.

THE BASICS

✉ Königstrasse 36
☎ 0331 969 42 00
🕐 Park: daily 7am–8pm. Schloss: Apr–Oct Tue–Sun 10–6; Nov–Dec, Mar Sat–Sun 10–4 (guided tours only)
🍴 Excellent restaurant
🚉 S-Bahn Wannsee, then bus 316
🚋 Tram 93 from Potsdam
💶 Inexpensive

SCHLOSS GLIENICKE

spsg.de

The mock-Renaissance schloss was designed in 1824 by Karl Friedrich Schinkel for Prince Friedrich Karl of Prussia, brother of Kaiser Wilhelm I. Nowadays the grounds are known for their arcadian follies and ornamental garden. The follies are by Schinkel, and the park was laid out by Peter Lenné, also responsible for Berlin's Tiergarten. Echoes of Renaissance Italy and Classical Greece can be detected among the follies. The most extraordinary flight of fancy must be the Klosterhof, containing artifacts from Venice and Pisa. Just outside the gate is Glienicker Brücke. The bridge came to the world's attention in 1962 when, marking the border between East and West, it was the scene of a prisoner swap involving the US pilot Gary Powers, who had been shot down by the Soviet air force on allegations of spying. The bridge subsequently starred in films and became a symbol of the Cold War.

Berlin caters to all, having a good selection of budget, mid-range and luxury hotels, as well as inexpensive hostels. If you're looking for a good-quality hotel, it's usually best to reserve a room well in advance.

Introduction

The steadily increasing number of visitors to Berlin has brought rapid growth and investment in the city's hotel industry, mainly in the luxury market. Good-quality mid-range and budget hotels tend to book up fast, but there is also an excellent selection of well-equipped hostels.

Location, Location

Budget hotels can be found virtually all over the city, with particular concentrations around Hackescher Markt, the lower end of Friedrichstrasse, Prenzlauer Berg, Kreuzberg (good for nightlife), Friedrichsfelde, Schöneberg and parts of Charlottenburg. They tend to be on side streets, but are never far from public transportation. This category includes *pensions*, which are smaller, often family-run places that offer bed and breakfast. Mid-range hotels cluster around Kurfürstendamm, Charlottenburg and the top end of Friedrichstrasse. Luxury hotels and business hotels are to be found around Unter den Linden, Kurfürstendamm, Savignyplatz and the middle section of Friedrichstrasse. Scenic, leafy outer locations include Wannsee, Grunewald and Müggelsee. Good transportation ensures quick transfers.

Breakfast Specials

Most hotels have a breakfast buffet, which can be simply *Kaffee und Schrippen* (coffee and rolls) with cheese and cold meats, or a feast of smoked meats, fresh fruit and cake. Breakfast is often not included in the price of a room in luxury and mid-range hotels, but is included in budget hotels and hostels.

FINDING A ROOM

Rooms can be booked in advance through the Berlin tourism website visitberlin.de or through the hotel finder at germany-tourism.de. The best place to start your search once you are in the city is at the nearest tourist office, which offers a room reservation service for a charge of €3 (free for phone bookings; tel 030 25 00 23 33).

Berlin caters to all accommodations needs, from simple hotels to grand, luxury establishments

Budget Hotels

PRICES

Expect to pay between €50 and €100 per night for a double room in a budget hotel.

ARTE LUISE KUNSTHOTEL

luise-berlin.com

Each room in this hotel has been individually designed by an artist. In a mansion dating from 1825, it has a striking facade, a lobby filled with sculptures and philosophical maxims decorating the stairway.

➕ J4 ✉ Luisenstrasse 19 ☎ 030 28 44 80 🚇 S- and U-Bahn Friedrichstrasse

H2

h-hotels.com

This large, modern hotel is in a prime central location with bus, tram and underground connections all close at hand. Rooms (some with disabled access) are air-conditioned, have TVs and free WiFi. The restaurant and on-site shop emphasize healthy eating.

➕ M4 ✉ Karl-Liebknecht-Strasse 32 ☎ 030 24 08 80 10 🚇 S- and U-Bahn Alexanderplatz

HOTEL AIR IN BERLIN

hotelairberlin.de

This medium-sized hotel enjoys a surprisingly quiet location, given its proximity to the Zoo and Ku'damm. Rooms are modern and comfortable; all are equipped with TVs, and some have a balcony or terrace. There are excellent transportation links to the sights.

➕ E7 ✉ Ansbacher Strasse 6 ☎ 030 212 99 20 🚇 U-Bahn Wittenbergplatz

HOTEL INGEBORG

hotelingeborg.de

Located in a quiet, upscale Charlottenburg side street, with easy access to Ku'damm shopping, this small, graceful hotel has just 10 simply furnished but clean rooms, decorated in bright, cheerful colors.

➕ C7 ✉ Wielandstrasse 33 ☎ 030 883 13 43 🚇 S-Bahn Savignyplatz, U-Bahn Adenauerplatz

HOTEL-PENSION FUNK

hotel-pensionfunk.de

Silent film star Asta Nielsen once lived in this elegant 1895 mansion. Many of the original art nouveau details have been preserved. Rooms are small but homey and good value for the location—and it's surprisingly quiet.

➕ D7 ✉ Fasanenstrasse 14a ☎ 030 882 71 93 🚇 U-Bahn Uhlandstrasse

HOTEL TRANSIT LOFT

transit-loft.de

For something a little different, book a stay in this converted factory in the heart of Prenzlauer Berg. There are bars and restaurants nearby and regular bus and tram services into town. The rooms are artfully designed, airy and well lit. Amenities include TV, free WiFi and a free breakfast buffet but no air conditioning.

➕ Off map M3 ✉ Immanuelkirchstrasse 14a ☎ 030 48 49 37 73 🚋 Tram M4

IBIS BERLIN HAUPTBAHNHOF HOTEL

accorhotels.com

Conveniently situated opposite the main station, this large, modern, no-smoking hotel has clean, comfortable rooms and offers a good breakfast buffet. The 24-hour reception and online check-in are added bonuses for travelers on a tight schedule.

➕ H4 ✉ Invalidenstrasse 53 ☎ 030 710 96 00 🚇 S- and U-Bahn Hauptbahnhof

Mid-Range Hotels

<table>
<tr><td>

PRICES

Expect to pay between €100 and €200 for per night for a double room in a mid-range hotel.

</td></tr>
</table>

ADINA APARTMENT HOTEL

adinahotels.com

Conveniently located in Mitte and close to the main station, this friendly hotel has studio rooms and apartments. There is also a swimming pool and restaurant.

➕ J3 ✉ Platz vor dem Neuen Tor 6 ☎ 030 200 03 20 🚇 S- and U-Bahn Hauptbahnhof

ART'OTEL BERLIN MITTE

artotel.de

This designer hotel has paintings by artist Georg Baselitz (b.1938) on the walls, a choice of red, green, blue or aubergine room tones, and international cuisine in the restaurant.

➕ L6 ✉ Wallstrasse 70–73 ✉ 030 24 06 20 🚇 U- and S-Bahn Friedrichstrasse

AZIMUT

azimuthotels.de

This hotel offers excellent service, clean and spacious rooms and is close to the action just off Kurfürstendamm. The rooftop café terrace is a great spot for admiring the view on a summer's evening.

➕ D7 ✉ Joachimstaler Strasse 39–40 ✉ 030 88 91 10 🚇 U-Bahn Kurfürstendamm

CIRCUS

circus-berlin.de

Circus has youthful verve, color and a highly individual, up-to-the-minute designer style, combined with a great quality to price ratio on both rooms and apartments.

➕ L3 ✉ Rosenthaler Strasse 1 ☎ 030 20 00 39 39 🚇 U-Bahn Rosenthaler Platz

THE DUDE BERLIN

thedudberlin.com

Housed in a graceful building dating from 1822, this welcoming hotel manages to be both close to the heart of the action in Mitte and tranquil at the same time. The rooms are bright and modern yet still retain an element of the house's original character.

➕ M6 ✉ Köpenicker Strasse 92 ☎ 030 411 98 81 77 🚇 U-Bahn Märkisches Museum

FJORD HOTEL

fjordhotelberlin.de

This modern, 64-room hotel on a quiet side street is convenient for Potsdamer Platz and the Kulturforum. In summer, you can breakfast on the roof terrace.

➕ H7 ✉ Bissingzeile 13 ☎ 030 52 68 54 🚇 U-Bahn Mendelssohn-Bartholdy-Park

HANSABLICK

hansablick.de

This welcoming, friendly hotel in a wonderful leafy setting, close to the River Spree and the Tiergarten yet only a few minutes' walk from the U-Bahn, has 50 bright, individually firnished rooms, all equipped with TVs and WiFi access. Some come with river views.

➕ E5 ✉ Flotowstrasse 6 ☎ 030 390 48 00 🚇 S-Bahn Tiergarten, U-Bahn Hansaplatz

HONIGMOND GARDEN HOTEL

honigmond.de

The main attraction of this small hotel in Scheunenviertel is its beautiful garden and intimate surroundings.

➕ J3 ✉ Invalidenstrasse 122 ☎ 030 28 44 55 77 🚇 S-Bahn Nordbahnhof

HOTEL HENRI

henri-hotels.com

Jugendstil architecture and antique furnishings are part of the attraction in this boutique hotel near Ku'damm. There is an American restaurant, the Brooklyn, here too.

⊞ D7 ✉ Meinekestrasse 9 ☎ 030 88 44 30
🚇 U-Bahn Kurfürstendamm

HOTEL KASTANIENHOF

kastanienhof.berlin

A friendly hotel with *Altberliner Charme* (Old Berlin charm) in a typical 19th-century apartment building, the Kastanienhof has 44 rooms decorated with historic photographs of the area.

⊞ L2 ✉ Kastanienallee 65 ☎ 030 44 30 50
🚇 U-Bahn Rosenthaler Platz

HOTEL-PENSION SAVOY

hotel-pension-savoy.de

The Savoy is off to the east in Kurfürstendamm. Each of the 20 guest rooms has modern amenities, including cable TV, telephone, hair dryer and safety deposit box, as well as a bathroom with bath or shower. It also offers bicycles to rent.

⊞ D7 ✉ Meinekestrasse 4 ☎ 030 88 47 16 10 🚇 U-Bahn Kurfürstendamm

HOTEL RIEHMERS HOFGARTEN

riehmers-hofgarten.de

This florid stucco apartment house was built in 1891 for wealthy Berliners. It has 20 good-size rooms as well as a smart restaurant.

⊞ J8 ✉ Yorckstrasse 83 ☎ 030 78 09 88 00
🚇 U-Bahn Mehringdamm

HOTEL VILLA KASTANIA

villakastania.de

Villa Kastania is a comfortable hotel in Charlottenburg. The 47 rooms have good facilities, and there is a pool.

⊞ Off map to west ✉ Kastanienallee 20
☎ 030 300 00 20 🚇 U-Bahn Theodor-Heuss-Platz

NH BERLIN-KURFÜRSTENDAMM

nh-hotels.com

This no-nonsense business hotel has immaculate rooms, a good standard of service and a central location. Facilities include a gym, a wellness zone and a couple of decent eateries.

⊞ D7 ✉ Grolmanstrasse 41–3 ☎ 030 88 42 60 🚇 U-Bahn Uhlandstrasse

NIKOLAI RESIDENCE

nikolai-residence.com

This small, modern hotel boasts a stunning location in the quaintly restored Nikolaiviertel, where the history of Berlin began. The rooms are spacious, pristine and well-lit, and there are lots of bars and restaurants close by.

⊞ L5 ✉ Am Nussbaum 5 ☎ 030 40 04 45 900 🚇 U-Bahn Klosterstrasse

RIVERSIDE ROYAL HOTEL AND SPA

riverside-mitte.de

All the rooms in this small hotel on the banks of the River Spree have been individually designed and decorated with antique furnishings, mirrors and chandeliers. Some have a great view over the river. There's a good Italian restaurant on site.

⊞ J4 ✉ Friedrichstrasse 105–106 ☎ 030 28 49 00 🚇 U- and S-Bahn Friedrichstrasse

TIERGARTEN BERLIN

hotel-tiergarten.de

Effortlessly combining the efficiency of a modern business hotel (with super-fast WiFi) with the charm of a privately owned lodging, the Tiergarten occupies an early 1900s building just north of the River Spree.

⊞ F4 ✉ Alt-Moabit 89 ☎ 030 39 98 96
🚇 U-Bahn Turmstrasse

Planning Ahead

When to Go

April to June is the most comfortable period to visit. Summer can be hot and humid. Expect rain at any time. The arts scene is liveliest between October and May. From late November to Christmas the city is resplendent with decorations and the streets are filled with markets.

TIME

Berlin is one hour ahead of the UK, six hours ahead of New York, and nine hours ahead of Los Angeles.

AVERAGE DAILY MAXIMUM TEMPERATURES

JAN	FEB	MAR	APR	MAY	JUN	JUL	AUG	SEP	OCT	NOV	DEC
36°F	37°F	46°F	55°F	66°F	72°F	75°F	73°F	68°F	55°F	45°F	37°F
2°C	3°C	8°C	13 °C	19°C	22°C	24°C	23°C	20°C	13°C	7°C	3°C

Spring (mid-March to May) is extremely pleasant, with flowers and trees coming into bloom throughout the parks and along the avenues.

Summer (June to early September) can be hot with the occasional dramatic thunder storm.

Fall (mid-September to November) is comfortable, but changeable with fine bright weather often preceded by periods of drizzle and grey skies.

Winter (December to mid-March) is extremely cold with occasional snowfalls, but it is common to experience crisp, bright days.

WHAT'S ON

On any given day, Berlin has around 250 exhibitions and more than 400 independent theater groups, 170 museums, 200 art galleries and 150 auditoriums. Check the listings magazines for details of events.

January 6-Day Race: Cycling event at the Velodrom, Landsberger Allee.

February International Film Festival (Berlinale): The world's filmmakers come to Potsdamer Platz.

May Karneval der Kulturen: Carnival of Cultures, Kreuzberg.

Lange Nacht der Museen: More than 100 museums are open after midnight.

June Fête de la Musique: Concerts (from rock to classical) at Mitte, Friedrichshain, Prenzlauer Berg, Kreuzberg and other open-air venues.

Christopher Street Day: Gay and lesbian procession.

September Musikfest: Three weeks of classical music concerts at various venues around the city.

September/October Berlin Marathon.

October German Unity Day (3 Oct): Street festivals on Unter den Linden.

November Jazz Festival Berlin: For five days, jazz concerts are held citywide.

December Christmas Markets: All month at Opernpalais (Unter den Linden 5), Breitscheidplatz, Gendarmenmarkt, Winterfeldtplatz (Sunday only), Schloss Charlottenburg, Potsdam and Spandau Altstadt.

New Year: Celebrations at the Brandenburg Gate and a gala evening at Staatsoper.

Berlin Online

visitberlin.de
The official site for the Berlin tourist board with details of hotels, sightseeing, guided tours and current events. You can order theater and concert tickets online and make hotel bookings from their list of approved hotels. Also in English.

awesomeberlin.de
A travel/lifestyle site with articles on topical subjects, insider tips, an events calendar and restaurant and entertainment listings.

berlin.de
The city of Berlin's official site with details of all the current events in both English and German.

uberlin.co.uk
Quirky expat website all in English, packed with unusual listings, fashion, music and insider tips.

freshmilk.de
A creative site dedicated to multimedia, modern art and culture.

tip-berlin.de
The official German-language site for the listings magazine *Tip*, detailing the major events and what is going on in the city in the way of films, music and partying in the month ahead.

zitty.de
In German only, the official site for the listings magazine *Zitty*, reviewing the top films, restaurants and bars in Berlin.

berlin-life.com
A locally produced online guide in English, with good what's-on and where-to-go information, and restaurant reviews.

bvg.de
Berlin public transportation site in English and German giving information on city travel.

TRAVEL SITES

fodors.com
A complete travel-planning site. You can research prices and weather; book air tickets, cars and rooms; ask questions (and get answers) from fellow travelers; and find links to other sites.

WIRED BERLIN

Visitors to the German capital can now expect free and unlimited internet access across large parts of the city. There are currently 650 wireless hotspots covering entire zones (for example Hackescher Markt, Gendarmenmarkt, Unter den Linden) as well as at major tourist sites like the Brandenburg Gate or the Fernsehturm. Museums are also covered, as are many stores, theaters and cinemas. For a full list of access points, including cafés, consult the website berlin.de.

Where coverage isn't available, there's Freifunk (free wirelss), a private initiative that operates at any number of tourist places, including Museums Island. Berlin's airports, the national rail network (Deutsche Bahn) and U-Bahn stations run by the local transport authority BVG all have their own systems in place.

Getting There

ENTRY REQUIREMENTS

For the latest passport and visa information, look up the embassy website at london.diplo.de. For latest information for visitors from the United States check the embassy website at germany.usembassy.gov

INSURANCE

EU nationals receive reduced-cost medical treatment with the EHIC card—obtain this card before traveling. Full health and travel insurance is still advised. US visitors should check their health coverage before departure and buy a supplementary policy as necessary.

AIRPORTS

Berlin is currently served by two airports: Tegel, to the northwest, and Schönefeld, to the southeast. The Schönefeld site is being expanded into a new airport, Berlin Brandenburg International, now scheduled to open in 2020.

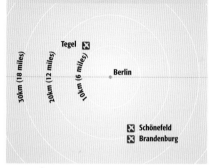

ARRIVING AT TEGEL AIRPORT

Tegel (TXL) is to the northwest of Berlin. For airport information, call 030 60 91 11 50. The airport is linked to the city via the bus network. Bus 109 from the airport will take you to Zoologischer Garten Station, as does bus X9. Bus 128 goes to the north of Berlin, while the TXL bus goes to Alexanderplatz. A taxi right into the city costs about €30 and takes 25–40 minutes depending on the traffic. For more information see berlin-airport.de.

ARRIVING AT SCHÖNEFELD AIRPORT

Schönefeld (SFX) is to the southeast, and for airport information, call 030 60 91 11 50. There is a free shuttle transfer from the terminal building to Berlin-Schönefeld airport station. The Airport Express takes passengers from the airport to the main rail station (Hauptbahnhof) and there are also S-Bahn and RegionalBahn trains (Regio). Buses X7, 162 and 171 link the terminal building with Rudow U-Bahn station. A taxi to the city costs about €50 and takes around 40 minutes. For more information see berlin-airport.de.

BERLIN BRANDENBURG INTERNATIONAL

The new high-tech airport being built next to the existing one at Schönefeld, 18km (11 miles) from Berlin city centre, is due to be completed late in 2020. It will have direct motorway access and a six-track rail station connecting directly into central Berlin and the surrounding region, and will handle all the region's air traffic; Tegel will close (but not Schönefeld). For more information, see berlin-airport.de.

ARRIVING BY BUS

The central bus station (Zentraler Omnibusbahnhof/ZOB, tel 030 30 10 01 75; zob-berlin/de) is on Masurenallee, opposite the International Conference Centre (ICC), in the district of Charlottenburg.

ARRIVING BY TRAIN

There are good connections from major European cities. The city's main station for international and long-distance services is Berlin Hauptbahnhof. The largest terminus on the European continent opened for business in 2006 and is constructed on three levels. Long-distance express trains arrive at the subterranean (*tief*) level and passengers leave via elevators or escalators. Several S-Bahn lines as well as regional trains depart form platforms on the first floor. The U-Bahn (U55 line only) is accessed over two levels. Note that there are two main exits: Washingtonplatz, handy for the Bundestag, and Europaplatz for trams and buses in the direction of Hackescher Markt and Alexanderplatz. For train information contact Deutsche Bahn (bahn.com; 00 44 8718 80 00 66; in the US 001 646 883 3264).

ARRIVING BY CAR

The A10/E55 ring road provides access to Berlin from all directions. If you intend to bring your car into central Berlin, it is a good idea to find a hotel with parking (preferably in advance) as there are few car parks and little on-street parking in and around the city.

CUSTOMS

Visiting from another EU country:
3,200 cigarettes or 400 cigarillos or 200 cigars or 3kg of smoking tobacco. 10 liters of spirits or 20 liters of fortified wine (such as port or sherry) or 90 liters of wine (of which only 60 liters can be sparkling wine) or 110 liters of beer.

Visiting Germany from outside the EU:
200 cigarettes or 100 cigarillos or 50 cigars or 250g of smoking tobacco. 1 liter of spirits or strong liqueurs. 2 liters of still table wine or 2 liters of fortified wine, spark-ling wine or other liqueurs. 50cc perfume. 250cc/ml of eau de toilette.

NEED TO KNOW GETTING THERE

Getting Around

POTSDAM BOUND

To do a side trip to historic Potsdam (▷ 104–105), the easiest way to get there under your own steam from the city is to take S-Bahn line S7. It passes through the heart of Berlin and you can catch it at stops that include Alexanderplatz, Hackescher Markt, Hauptbahnhof and Zoologischer Garten. Note: you must have a ticket that covers Zone C.

VISITORS WITH DISABILITIES

Make sure you download the free app accessBerlin. This indicates the best routes through the city for visitors with limited mobility, as well as accessible attractions and sights. Use the filter to function to check disabled access in hotels, restaurants and other public places, and the location of public restrooms.

Buses have rear-door access (assisted by driver) and safety straps for wheelchairs.

Berlin has an excellent public transport network, with two urban rail services and bus and tram routes. The local transport authority is the Berliner Verkehrsbetriebe (BVG).

● BVG Information Service. For timetables and tickets call 030 194 49 or visit bvg.de.

● S-Bahn Berlin GmbH Information Service s-bahn-berlin.de

TYPES OF TICKET

● The 24-hour ticket (*Tageskarte*) and the weekly *7-Tage-Karte* allow unlimited travel on the BVG network (trains, buses, trams and the ferry from Wannsee to Kladow). The weekly ticket covers unlimited travel during any seven-day period from validation until midnight on the seventh day.

● A single one-way ticket (*Einzelfahrausweis*) is valid for two hours. You can transfer or interrupt your travel.

● The *Kurzstrecke* (short-distance ticket) is valid on the U- and S-Bahn for up to three stops including transfers, or for six stops only (bus/tram).

● BerlinWelcomeCard entitles one adult and up to three children age 6–14 to free BVG travel for two–six days as well as reductions on sight-seeing trips, museums and theaters. Ask at your hotel, tourist information offices or U-Bahn ticket offices.

● Children under 14: reduced-rate travel; children under 6: free.

THE METRO

● The U-Bahn (subway) and S-Bahn (city railway) are interchangeable.

● You must buy a ticket from station foyers or from vending machines on platforms. Validate your ticket at a machine on the platform before boarding the train. Routes are referred to by the final stop on the line.

● Trains run every 5 or 10 minutes, Mon–Fri 5am–1am (U-Bahn) or 5am–1.30am (S-Bahn). On weekends there is a 24-hour service on U- and S-Bahn lines.

• You may take bicycles on the U-Bahn on weekdays between 9am and 2pm and after 5.30pm, and all weekend. Cyclists may travel on the S-Bahn at any time. You will need to buy a bicycle ticket.

BUSES
• Central Bus Station is at Funkturm (tel 030 30 10 01 75; zob.berlin).
• Enter double-decker buses at the front and leave by the doors in the middle or at the back. Pay the driver with small change or show your ticket (see above). Multiple-use tickets, also valid for U- and S-Bahn, can be bought from vending machines at some bus stops or at U-Bahn stations, but not from the driver.
• Routes 100 and 200 are particularly useful, linking the West End with Unter den Linden and Alexanderplatz (▷ panel, right).
• More than 70 night buses operate half-hourly from 1am to 4am. Night buses are marked with the prefix "N".

STRASSENBAHNEN (TRAMS)
• Trams operate largely in eastern Berlin as far as the main rail station (Hauptbahnhof). Tickets are available from vending machines inside the trams. Metro trams (marked with prefix "M") run through the night at 30-minute intervals.

MAPS AND TIMETABLES
• Obtain timetables and maps from large U-Bahn ticket offices such as Alexanderplatz (tel 030 19 449; bvg.de).

TAXIS
• Taxis are reasonable value, with stands throughout the city. Only use cabs with a meter.
• There is a small surcharge for baggage.
• Not all drivers know their way, so travel with your own map.
• The central taxi phone number is 030 44 33 222; other useful numbers include the chauffeur service (030 44 04 40) and bike taxis (velotaxis, 030 93 95 83 46).

BVG FERRIES
BVG ferry lines in the Wannsee, Treptow and Köpenick areas include services from Wannsee to Alt-Kladow (departs hourly, journey time 20 minutes), Grünau to Wendenschloss and around the Müggelsee.

TOUR BUSES
For the cost of a single bus ticket (*Einzelfahrschein*), you can access most of Berlin's sights from the top of a double-decker bus, hopping on and off as and where you wish. Buses 100, 200 depart from Zoologischer Garten (opposite McDonalds) every 10 minutes. Bus 100 stops include the Siegessäule, Bundestag, Brandenburger Tor, Unter den Linden, Museumsinsel and Alexanderplatz, while the 200 service takes in Kulturforum, Potsdamer Platz, Freidrichstrasse and Gendarmenmarkt. Ticets are valid (one way) on both services interchangeably.

NEED TO KNOW GETTING AROUND

Essential Facts

EMBASSIES IN BERLIN

- Spain
- ✉ Lichtensteinallee 1
- ☎ 030 25 40 070
- Portugal
- ✉ Zimmerstrasse 56
- ☎ 030 59 03 500
- United Kingdom
- ✉ Wilhelmstrasse 70–71
- ☎ 030 20 45 70
- United States
- ✉ Pariser Platz 2
- ☎ 030 83 050

EUROS

The euro is the official currency of Germany. Bank notes come in denominations of € 5, 10, 20, 50, 100, 200 and 500; and coins in denominations of 1, 2, 5, 10, 20 and 50 cents and € 1 and 2.

CUSTOMS REGULATIONS

For details of duty-free allowances for visitors from within the EU and from countries outside the EU, see list given in the "Customs" panel on page 117.

ELECTRICITY

- Standard supply is 230 volts. Sockets take two-round-pin plugs.

LOST PROPERTY

- At Rudolfstrasse 1–8 (Friedrichshain) or Platz der Luftbrücke 6 (tel 030 90 27 73 101)
- BVG Transport Lost and Found (Fündburo), Potsdamer Strasse 180–182, tel 030 19 44 9

MEDICINES

- Take any specially prescribed medications with you. Check on the generic name of any drugs before you leave home, in case you need to replace your prescription while away.

MEDICAL AND DENTAL TREATMENT

- There are plenty of English-speaking doctors in Berlin. For a referral service telephone the medical emergency number.
- Emergency numbers (within Berlin): medical: 01804 22 55 23 62; dental: 030 89 00 43 33.
- EU citizens receive free health care (excluding dental care) on production of their EHIC card, but private medical insurance is still advised and is essential for all other visitors.

MONEY MATTERS

- Exchange offices (*Wechselstuben*) can be found all over Berlin: Hauptbahnhof (main station, open daily 7.30am–10pm); Friedrichstrasse station (open Mon–Fri 7am–8pm, Sat–Sun 8–8).
- ATMs can be found citywide.

OPENING HOURS

- Shops are usually open Mon–Fri 9.30–8, Sat 10–8. Some shops may open 24 hours.

- Banks open Mon–Fri 9.30–3, but afternoons may vary. Some banks close over lunch.
- Pharmacies open Mon–Fri 9.30–6.30, Sat 9–2. Call 030 31 00 31 for night pharmacies.

STUDENT VISITORS
- Discounts on public transport, in museums and some theaters are available with an International Student Identity Card.
- European youth passes are also available for people under 26.

SENSIBLE PRECAUTIONS
- Although Berlin is one of the safer European cities, always remain on your guard. Keep a close eye on bags and do not hang them on the back of chairs in restaurants.
- Avoid poorly lighted areas. Some places such as Motzstrasse can become seedy red-light districts at night.
- Keep wallets and purses concealed when travelling on the U-Bahn and trams.

SIGHTSEEING TOURS
- BBS Berliner Bären Stadtrundfahrt: Daily tours and days out in eight languages. Departures from Ku'damm and Alexanderplatz (tel 030 35 19 52 70).
- Berolina Stadtrundfahrten: Daily bus tours of Berlin and Potsdam–Sanssouci in eight languages. Departures from Ku'damm at Meinekestrasse (tel 030 88 56 80 30).
- Berlin by boat: Starting from close to the Berliner Dom, you can take a boat tour along the River Spree through "historical Berlin" (tel 030 53 63 600; sternundkreis.de). Tours run daily and last one hour.

TELEPHONES
- Pink phone booths marked with a "T" take prepaid cards, sold in post offices, gas stations and newspaper kiosks. They are located outside main transport hubs and other central locations.
- Boxes marked "International" and telephones in post offices are for long-distance calls.

EMERGENCY PHONE NUMBERS
- Coins are not needed for emergency calls from public telephones: Police ☎ 110; Fire and Ambulance ☎ 112
- Berliner Krisendienst (☎ 030 390 63 10; berliner-krisendienst.de) provides round-the-clock emergency counselling in English and German.

NEED TO KNOW ESSENTIAL FACTS

PUBLIC HOLIDAYS

● 1 January; Good Friday; Easter Monday; 1 May; Ascension Day; Pentecost Monday; 3 October (German Unity Day); Christmas Day; 26 December.

POST OFFICES

● ✉ Potsdamer Platz 2 🕐 Mon–Thu 8am–8.30pm, Fri 8–8, Sat 9–5 ✉ Bahnhof Friedrichstrasse, Georgenstrasse 12 🕐 Mon–Fri 6–10, Sat–Sun 8–10
● Stamps can be bought from vending machines as well as from post offices.
● Postboxes are bright yellow.

● Calls are cheapest after 10pm and on Sunday.
● Follow the dialling instructions (in several languages) in the box.
● To call the UK from Berlin dial 0044, then omit the first 0 from the area code.
● To call Berlin from the UK dial 0049 30, then the number.
● To call the US from Berlin dial 001.
● To call Berlin from the US dial 01149 30, then the number.
● For local information: 11833; for international information: 11834

TOILETS
● Men's toilets are labelled *Herren*, women's *Damen* or *Frauen*.
● Public restrooms can be found all over the city. You have to pay to use them, but they are clean and well kept.

TOURIST INFORMATION OFFICES
● Berlin Tourismus Marketing, Am Karlsbad 11 (tel 030 25 00 23 33; visitberlin.de).
● Berlin Hauptbahnhof, main rail station, Ground Floor, North Entrance, Europlatz 1, open daily 8am–9pm.
● Europa-Center Tauentzienstrasse 9, open Mon–Sat 10–8.
● Brandenburger Tor, South Wing, Pariser Platz, open Apr–Oct daily 9.30am –7pm; Nov–Mar 9.30am–6pm.
● Fernsehturm, Panoramastrasse 1a, open daily Mon–Sat 7am–9pm, Sun 8–6.

WOMEN TRAVELERS
● Berlin is generally a safe city for women traveling alone and harassment of any kind is rare. Avoid poorly lit streets at night as you would in any city.
● Frauenzentrum Schokofabrik (Mariannenstrasse 6; tel 030 615 29 99; frauenzentrum-schokofabrik.de) is a social center exclusively for women with dance and sport facilities, a Turkish bath and café.

Language

BASICS

ja	yes
nein	no
bitte	please
danke	thank you
guten Morgen	good morning
guten Abend	good evening
gute Nacht	good night
auf Wiedersehen	goodbye
heute	today
gestern	yesterday
morgen	tomorrow
die Speisekarte	menu
das Frühstück	breakfast
das Mittagessen	lunch
das Abendessen	dinner
der Weisswein	white wine
der Rotwein	red wine
das Bier	beer
das Brot	bread
die Milch	milk
der Zucker	sugar
das Wasser	water
die Rechnung	check (bill)
das Zimmer	room
offen	open
geschlossen	closed
wieviel?	how much?
teuer	expensive
billig	cheap
sprechen Sie Englisch?	do you speak English?
Ich spreche kein Deutsch	I don't speak German
Ich verstehe nicht	I don't understand
Entschuldigen Sie	Excuse me
der Bahnhof	train station
der Flughafen	airport
die Bank	bank
das Postamt	post office
die Polizei	police
das Krankenhaus	hospital

USEFUL WORDS

klein	small
gross	large
schnell	quickly
kalt	cold
warm	hot
gut	good

Timeline

A BERLIN FIRST

Werner Siemens and Johann Georg Malske manufactured the first telegraph in a house on Schöneberger Strasse.

THE WALL

In 1961 200,000 people escaped the GDR in the East and fled to the West, 152,000 of them via Berlin. On the night of 12 August 1961 the GDR closed the border, erecting a wall of barbed wire, concrete slabs and stones. This was followed by the building of the Wall, a concrete structure 12km (7.5 miles) long. The border was heavily guarded and during the time the Wall stood 152 people lost their lives trying to escape.

Left to right: Frederick the Great; logo of the Socialist Unity Party, ruling party of the GDR; Hitler enters the Sudetenland, 1938; WW II commemorative plaques at the Olympic Stadium; signs at former Checkpoint Charlie; entrance to the Olympic Stadium

1244 First recorded mention of Berlin.

1359 Berlin becomes a member of the Hanseatic League trading association.

1443 Frederick II of Brandenburg builds the first Berlin castle (Schloss).

1618–48 Berlin is devastated by Austrian and Swedish armies during the Thirty Years' War. The population is halved to less than 6,000.

1701 Elector Frederick III proclaims himself King Frederick I of Prussia. In 1740 Frederick the Great becomes king.

1806 Napoleon enters Berlin.

1848 Germany's "bourgeois revolution" sees demands for greater middle-class representation in government.

1871 Berlin becomes the capital of a united German Empire under Kaiser Wilhelm I and his Chancellor, Prince Otto von Bismarck.

1918 After the end of World War I, Kaiser Wilhelm II abdicates to make way for a German Republic.

1920s Despite growing social and economic instability, Berlin becomes a cultural powerhouse. Grosz, Einstein, Brecht and Gropius flourish.

1933 Hitler becomes German Chancellor.

1936 Berlin hosts the Olympic Games in a new, purpose-built stadium.

1938 On the "night of breaking glass" the Nazis orchestrate the destruction of Jewish properties and synagogues.

1939–45 World War II.

1945 Berlin lies in ruins, its population reduced from 4 million to 2.8 million.

1945–89 A city divided (▷ side panel).

1989 On 9 November the collapse of communism in Eastern Europe leads to the opening of the Berlin Wall and its eventual demise.

1990 Germany is unified.

2000 Berlin once again becomes the capital of a united Germany.

2006 The Olympiastadion hosts the soccer world cup final.

2014 The 25th anniversary of the fall of the Berlin Wall marked with celebrations and fireworks.

2019 The old Prussian Stadtschloss palace comes to life as the Humboldt Forum, an ambitious museum complex.

A CITY DIVIDED

1945 Berlin is divided into four zones of occupation, administered by French, British, US and Soviet forces.

1948–49 A Soviet attempt to force the Western Allies to withdraw from Berlin by blockading the city is foiled by a gigantic airlift of supplies.

1949 Germany is divided into the Federal Republic and the communist German Democratic Republic. Berlin is stranded in the GDR.

1953 Construction workers in East Berlin, protesting at low wages, provoke a full-scale uprising, which is put down by Soviet tanks.

1961 The flood of East Germans to the West is staunched by the building of the Berlin Wall.

1963 John F. Kennedy demonstrates American support for West Berlin in his famous "Ich bin ein Berliner" speech.

Index

Titles in the Series

- Amsterdam
- Bangkok
- Barcelona
- Berlin
- Boston
- Brussels and Bruges
- Budapest
- Chicago
- Dubai
- Dublin
- Edinburgh
- Florence
- Hong Kong
- Istanbul
- Krakow
- Las Vegas
- Lisbon
- London
- Madrid
- Melbourne
- Milan
- Montréal
- Munich
- New York City
- Orlando
- Paris
- Rome
- San Francisco
- Seattle
- Shanghai
- Singapore
- Sydney
- Tokyo
- Toronto
- Venice
- Vienna
- Washington, D.C.